Flash™ 99% Good: A Guide to Macromedia Flash™ Usability

About the Authors

Kevin Airgid is an interactive designer who has concentrated in the interactive field for many years. He has worked exclusively in interactive design since the inception of Mosaic, the first graphical web browser. Kevin's previous experience includes designing multimedia projects such as CD-ROM, touch-screen kiosks, and graphic user interfaces for interactive television and the Web.

Kevin has extensive experience designing web sites for various Fortune 500 companies, using Macromedia, Flash, and Shockwave. He has created multimedia projects for the Detroit Tigers, Siemens, Toyota, Bell Canada, Marriott Hotel, Amnesty International, and GM, including Cadillac and Chevrolet.

Kevin is the recipient of several design awards and he has been featured in the Macromedia Flash Showcase. Kevin holds a degree in visual arts from the University of Western Ontario and lives in Ontario, Canada.

You can visit Kevin's web site at http://www.airgid.com.

Stephanie Reindel is an information architect with a broad background in the field of user experience design. She has extensive experience in developing information architectures and evaluating the usability of interactive products, including web sites, software applications, kiosks, and interactive multimedia products. Stephanie has performed usability studies and developed information architectures for a variety of well-known clients including Toyota, Ford Motor Company, Siemens Automotive, The American Iron and Steel Institute, Amnesty International, and ePrize.

Stephanie holds a bachelor's degree in marketing from the University of Michigan, with a minor in psychology. Additional industry experience includes advertising, marketing, public relations, and communications.

Flash™ 99% Good: A Guide to Macromedia Flash™ Usability

Kevin Airgid
Stephanie Reindel

McGraw-Hill/Osborne

New York / Chicago / San Francisco / Lisbon
London / Madrid / Mexico City / Milan / New Delhi
San Juan / Seoul / Singapore / Sydney / Toronto

McGraw-Hill/Osborne
2600 Tenth Street
Berkeley, California 94710
U.S.A.

To arrange bulk purchase discounts for sales promotions, premiums, or fund-raisers, please contact
McGraw-Hill/Osborne at the above address. For information on translations or book distributors outside the
U.S.A., please see the International Contact Information page immediately following the index of this book.

Flash™ 99% Good: A Guide to Macromedia Flash™ Usability

1234567890 WCT WCT 0198765432

ISBN 0-07-222287-5

Publisher	**Proofreader**
Brandon Nordin	Paul Tyler
Vice President & Associate Publisher	**Indexer**
Scott Rogers	David Heiret
Acquisitions Editor	**Computer Designer**
Jim Schachterle	Kelly Stanton-Scott
Project Editor	**Illustrators**
Janet Walden	Michael Mueller, Lyssa Wald
Acquisitions Coordinator	**Series Design**
Timothy Madrid	Kelly Stanton-Scott
Technical Editor	**Cover Design**
Tina Miletich	Pattie Lee, Greg Scott
Copy Editor	
Marcia Baker	

This book was composed with Corel VENTURA™ Publisher.

I dedicate this book to my wife for all her support and positive feedback.
 –*Kevin*

To my husband Brian—I dedicate this book to you for the love, support, and patience you've shown me throughout the process of writing this book. You are my inspiration and my reward. I love you.
 –*Stephanie*

Two are better than one … for if they fall, one will lift up the other.
 –*Ecclesiastes 4:9–10*

Contents at a Glance

Contents

1 Yin and Yang of Design and Usability 1

2 Design and Usability: The Pros and Cons 17

3   Know Your Goal, Know Your Audience   41

4   Flash Navigation: The Good, the Bad, and the Ugly   77

Acknowledgments

Kevin & Stephanie:

We would like to say thank you to the many people who have contributed their ideas, expertise, and experience to the writing of this book. Many have taken the time to provide us with interviews and others have graciously allowed us to use their web sites to illustrate points and ideas throughout this book. We sincerely appreciate each and every contribution that helped make the writing of this book possible.

We would also like to say thank you to Jim Schachterle, Tim Madrid, and the rest of the team at McGraw-Hill/Osborne for all of their help and patience with writing this book, and to thank our technical editor, Tina Miletich, for her excellent suggestions and comments.

Stephanie:

Writing this book has been a wonderful experience. I am grateful for the opportunity to say thank you to a few of the many who have taught me, inspired me, and just plain put up with me.

First and foremost, I would like to thank God for giving me the ability and opportunity to write this book. I owe all that I am, all that I have, and all that I've accomplished to the goodness and grace of my Heavenly Father.

I would like to say thank you to Lou Rosenfeld and Keith Instone for taking the time to provide input for this book based on their many years of professional experience.

I would also like to thank my friend and former coworker, Kristen Truong, for the time she spent sharing her experience and "showing me the ropes" when I was new to the field of information architecture.

To my friend, coworker, and coauthor Kevin Airgid—thank you for your willingness to listen to my ideas and opinions, and for resisting the urge to hang up the phone on me in the middle of one of my many "usability spiels."

Finally, I would like to thank my husband Brian for putting up with me for the past few months while I spent many late nights "accomplishing" this book. Thank you for the encouragement you've provided and for "cracking the whip" when I needed it.

Introduction

This book was written in an effort to help extinguish the idea that Flash and usability cannot coexist. There is an all-too-common battle between creative designers/developers and information architects/usability experts when it comes to the use of Flash in web site design. For the many who have been involved in such a battle, we feel your pain. It's been said that usability experts are from Mars and graphic designers are from Venus. We hope that by providing some useful insight into both worlds—the design world and the usability world—you'll come away with a better understanding of where each side is coming from and how the two can work together and get along.

Who Should Read This Book

This book is geared mainly toward Flash designers and developers, however, anyone involved in a project that incorporates Flash would benefit from reading it. This includes information architects, usability experts, project managers, sales/account managers, and even clients.

If you're interested in expanding your knowledge on how to use Flash to design and develop sites that people enjoy using, read this book. If you want to intelligently answer your client's critical questions about the appropriateness of Flash for their site, read this book. If you never thought the words "Flash" and "usable" could learn to get along, read this book. We're out to show you that form and function can coexist, and that, when used appropriately, Flash is 99% *good*.

How to Read This Book

This book is best read anywhere. You needn't be sitting behind a computer surfing the Web to understand the chapters because screen captures of the sites we reference are provided.

Important to note is throughout the book we refer primarily to web sites; however, the ideas and techniques presented can be applied to virtually any interactive medium that incorporates the use of Flash, such as software applications, CD-ROMS, and kiosks.

Another important note to make is we use the terms "information architecture" and "usability" interchangeably. While we recognize the fundamental differences between the two, we chose not to differentiate in this book because the common end goal of each is to enhance and ensure an overall positive user experience.

Because this isn't a "how to" book, we refer several times to web sites where you can find additional information on how to accomplish various Flash techniques and effects. For your convenience, we compiled a list of additional resource links in a central location at **http:// www.flash99good.com**.

Special Features

This book features interviews with top experts in the fields of Flash design, information architecture, and web site usability. These interviews open a glimpse into the thoughts and professional experience of some of the most talented Flash developers, information architects, and usability experts in the world. We conclude the book with an interview from Kevin Lynch, the chief software architect of Macromedia, on the future of Flash.

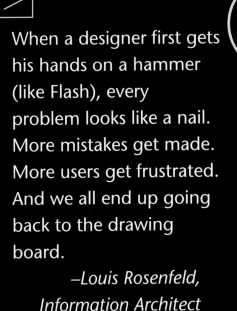

When a designer first gets his hands on a hammer (like Flash), every problem looks like a nail. More mistakes get made. More users get frustrated. And we all end up going back to the drawing board.

—Louis Rosenfeld,
Information Architect

chapter

Yin and Yang of Design and Usability

In this chapter, we introduce some of the basic ideas and theories behind design and usability. Throughout this chapter and the remainder of the book, we refer mainly to design and usability as they relate to web sites. The ideas presented and discussed might be applied to any digital interactive product that incorporates Flash, however, including software, software applications, kiosk displays, and CD/DVD-ROMs. The objective is not to tell you how to design or to present you with a black-and-white list of usability do's and don'ts. We won't go into minute detail about each and every usability or design standard that exists— numerous other books already do that well. Instead, we choose to highlight a few of the key standards and theories that, in our experience, seem to cause the most conflict between the designer and usability expert (also known as the information architect), especially in relation to Flash design. We provide some basic guidelines to remember as you design, each of which is covered in much greater detail later in the book. We hope you take away what you need to design highly creative and usable Flash products that attract, engage, and retain users by providing them with a positive experience.

What Is Usability?

Usability is a term relevant to any product with which users must interact. At its most basic level, *usability* refers to the connection between a product and its users, and is directly related to a product's usefulness. For a product to be useful it must enable users to accomplish their goals in an effective, efficient manner. Usability is not the end goal in and of itself; instead, it's a means to an end.

According to the International Organization for Standardization, usability can be defined as "the extent to which a product can be used by specified users to achieve specified goals with effectiveness, efficiency, and satisfaction in a specified context of use" (ISO 9241-11).

The same standards hold true for web sites, software applications, and other digital interactive products. The intended users of these products must be able to accomplish their goals and satisfy their needs in a way that either meets or exceeds their expectations for the product to be deemed "usable."

As a whole, four factors—focus, function, flow, and feeback—determine the usability of a product.

) *Focus* refers to how well the content and information meets the users' needs and expectations.

) *Function* refers to how well each element of the product works in relation to the needs and goals of the user.

) *Flow* refers to how well processes and applications (such as a check-out process on an e-commerce site) fit the needs and goals of the user.

) *Feedback* refers to how well the system responds to the actions of the user, usually through instruction and information, to facilitate the completion of tasks and goals.

Usability is the characteristic that incorporates each of these factors, resulting in a product that's purposeful, understandable, error tolerable, and ultimately useful.

Why Is Usability So Important?

When users choose to visit a web site, they do so with a set of goals in mind—goals that typically involve satisfying a desire or need. For instance, a user might visit an e-commerce site with the goal of purchasing a birthday present for a sibling. Or a user might visit a medical information web site with the goal of finding the symptoms to a particular disease to determine whether they should see a doctor. When users can accomplish what they set out to do, they will equate the achievement of their goals with a positive experience. In contrast, users will attribute difficulty in trying to accomplish their goals or the inability to achieve them altogether to a negative overall experience.

The Cost of Poor Usability

Perhaps the best way to look at why usability is important is to look at the consequences of a negative user experience resulting from poor usability. Most users won't return to a web site on which they've suffered a negative experience. In a world where people lack patience and have come to expect instant gratification, the Internet has become another means of providing just that. Many users choose to visit a web site because they assume it will be either more efficient (quicker) or more effective for achieving their goals than the available alternatives. When usability problems challenge this assumption, users become frustrated and begin seeking alternatives, often in the form of competitive sites and products. Failure to provide useful content and functionality is estimated to result in a loss of roughly 40 percent of repeat visitors and 50 percent of lost online sales. In addition, numerous studies in which Flash sites were compared to an HTML counterpart found the use of Flash typically lowers usability.

Usability is equally important in other types of interactive products, such as software applications. Companies and individuals typically choose to use a particular piece of software or software application because they expect that by doing so, they'll become more productive. Usability deficiencies can quickly disprove this theory, resulting in productivity levels at or below where they were before implementing the software. Users don't have the time or patience to "figure out" unusable software and typically choose an alternative means to accomplish their goal—either through a competitor's product or by reverting to the way they did things previously.

In the long run, poor usability can lead to lost sales, broken customer relationships, reduced productivity, and increased costs, all of which will ultimately result in the failure of the product or system.

The Branding Effect

Branding involves more than just making sure users recognize and relate to a product name or logo. *Branding* involves creating an emotional connection between the users and the product or site. Because web sites are interactive rather than passive, users attribute emotions directly to their experiences on the site. This experience triggers either positive or negative emotions, which, in turn, influence the users' perception of the brand image portrayed on the site.

The underlying goal of creating a strong brand image is to attract, engage, and retain customers. Although good usability alone won't typically attract new users or customers (marketing communications and advertising tools are much more effective for that), once a user is attracted it's essential for them to have a positive experience to engage them (keep them interested) and retain them (keep them coming back). And, in some instances, a web site's usability features can be used in marketing and advertising messages as a consumer benefit to help those mediums attract new users.

When applied correctly, Flash can be an effective tool for engaging and retaining users. With it, designers can highlight products and other important elements, reinforce navigation, and create helpful tools like interactive tutorials. When used incorrectly for things like lengthy intros, mystifying navigation, and annoying, unstoppable audio, then Flash becomes a nuisance, leaving users with a bad taste in their mouths. A negative user experience will directly (and negatively) affect how users perceive the company, product, and brand. When users associate a negative brand image with a product, they aren't likely to remain users of that product for long. For a business site this means lost business and lost sales, which in turn lead to reduced profitability. An unusable site can actually be worse than no site at all.

A Usable Brand: eBay.com

Behind nearly every successful online brand, you'll find a usable web site. eBay (http://www .ebay.com) is one of the best examples of this type of online branding success. A few years ago, if you walked up to someone on the street and asked if they'd heard of eBay, you might well have gotten a blank stare and a response such as, "e-who?". Today, you can ask nearly anyone if they've heard of eBay and their answer will probably be something more like "Oh, yeah, that online auction site. I found the neatest …"

Why is eBay so successful? After all, it doesn't have the coolest-looking site around. No Flash intros, no funky music playing, no eye-catching animations—all in all, just a regular, almost visually boring site. What it does have, though, is an extremely easy-to-use site that enables its users to accomplish their goals, usually selling or buying, quickly and efficiently. Given the diversity of eBay's target audience, this is quite an achievement. eBay is used by countless thousands of people from around the world—male and female, teenagers to senior citizens, Internet geniuses to Internet novices, users of 486 PCs to Power Mac G4s and 28.8 modems to T1 lines, all with a vast array of backgrounds, interests, and lifestyles. Imagine what the story might have been like if eBay had ignored its users and focused on using cutting-edge design technology and creative gimmicks to give its site more pizzazz. This strategy might have satisfied the needs of its ultracreative, Internet-savvy, broadband connection users, but the vast majority of eBay's users would have been left in the wake, unable to accomplish their auction buying and selling goals. eBay became an online branding success by finding the common needs and goals, in relation to the goals of its auction business, among a disparate group of users and by developing a site focused on meeting those needs and goals.

Achieving Maximum Usability

The key to achieving maximum usability lies in knowing the goals of the site as well as the goals of the user. Ask yourself, why are valuable time and resources being spent on this site? What goal are we trying to accomplish? What are we going to provide? Whether the goal of your site is to sell products or to provide information on a specific topic, or to show off your own personal talents and abilities, you need to define the criteria for success. If you don't understand why your site exists, neither will your users.

Once you define the goals of your site, you can begin to identify your target users. You can start by asking yourself questions like "Why would someone want to spend valuable time visiting this site? What are their goals? What do they need to accomplish?" If you can't answer these questions, then perhaps you need to reassess your purpose for having the site in the first place. If you can't come up with a reason for users to visit your site, neither will they. Once you do answer these questions, however, you can begin to identify the types of people who might have one or many of these goals. These are your target users, those for whom you are ultimately designing the site and those who will ultimately determine the success or failure of your site.

Web sites and software products provide a means-to-an-end goal. Users expect that this means will be faster, easier, more interesting, or better in some other way than an alternative means would have been in accomplishing their goal. The path to attainment of that goal makes up an experience, either good or bad. Usability is achieved in understanding the people who will be having the experience, identifying the goals they're trying to accomplish, and uniting these users and their goals within an engaging design.

Who's Responsible for Achieving Usability?

In many ways, each person involved in the design and development of a web site holds some portion of the responsibility for achieving a usable product. For example, *graphic designers* are responsible for incorporating creative content such as color, graphics, and multimedia elements in a way that enhances, rather than hinders, usability. *Programmers* are responsible for making sure the site functions properly, so users can complete processes without encountering errors or defects. But it usually falls on the shoulders of the information architect to make sure the product as a whole is, indeed, usable.

Information architecture is a key component of the design process for creating a usable interactive product. *Information architecture* is the process of organizing and labeling content, designing navigation systems, and modeling information process flows that help people find and manage information more successfully. The *information architect* is the primary advocate for the users and takes into account the users' needs, goals, expectations, and abilities to create a successful information structure, one that provides users with a satisfying experience.

To create this structure, information architects work with input from a variety of other disciplines. For example, they often rely on the marketing scheme and target audiences to identify key user groups and guide development of user goals. In designing the information flow on the site, a programmer might provide input on technical feasibility and implications. In designing navigation, organization, and labeling systems, designers are consulted for their creative input on the most ideal integration. In the end, the information architect ties together user needs and goals, technical viability, and creative content design, all against the backdrop of the company's goals to create a product that provides users with a positive experience.

The Information Architect's Perspective on Design

An information architect's key focus is the experience of the user, and rightly so, because that's their expertise. An information architect's job is to act as the voice of the user. Whether the product is a web site, CD/DVD-ROM, software application, or some other form of interactive media, the information architect is charged with the task of ensuring that the audience the product is intended for can use it and finds it useful. Sometimes this means *not* incorporating the latest, most cutting-edge design technology on every page of a site. Sometimes it means limiting the extent of graphics and creativity that can be applied because of the limitations and needs of the intended users. This doesn't mean information architects are antidesign or unappreciative of its value. It simply isn't their focal point or forte.

Although the ideas and principles behind information architecture have been around for quite some time, the term "information architect" has only gained popularity in the past few years. I first became familiar with the term when I was working for a large advertising agency as an account supervisor, overseeing the Internet division of a large automotive account. I was managing a project for a web site that would, ultimately, be viewed and used by millions of people. At the time, no information architects were at the company—just the typical (or typical at the time) development team consisting of a creative director, graphic designer, programmer, and project manager. The designer I was working with on this particular project was one who knew Flash (not every designer did at the time) and wanted to take this as an opportunity to show off his skills. He created a site entirely in Flash. The site was confined to a window the size of a 3×5 card and, on first (and second and third …) view, seemed to lack any navigation entirely.

When I reviewed the site in its early stages, my first reaction went something like, "Wow—that's a really cool design, but what do I do once I'm here? Where's the navigation? Everything on the page is moving, but I don't see any place to click!" It was quickly pointed out that the navigation was embodied in a set of moving, blinking, letterlike elements that came and went in a random fashion. Only by accidentally moving my mouse over one of these "letters" as it was heading for the edge of the page did I realize this element was "clickable." I clicked and was taken to another equally eventful page. It was here I realized the letter I'd clicked on represented a navigation label. "Oh, I get it," I thought, "hmm … let's see, how do I go back to that page I was on … wait a second, what happened to the Back button?" No Back button. It was gone, missing in action, and nowhere to be found. I gave up, and all too easily, according to the designer, who claimed this type of fun-house style, smoke-and-mirrors navigation is what users want. "Users are bored with the typical navigation that's out there," I heard him say. "They like to hunt for navigation … it adds an element of mystery to the site." I'm not kidding—this is what he told me. Maybe you're not surprised. Maybe you've even said the same thing. But my gut reaction to this statement was the designer was horribly wrong and this site would frustrate users so much they would give up like I did and never come back.

Unfortunately, and much to my dismay, the creative director (the designer's boss) was in complete agreement with him. And even in my high-and-mighty position as the account supervisor (much humor intended), it seemed I had little say-so in the matter because all I had at the time was my own humble gut-level opinion. But I wasn't about to give in that easily. I decided to do a little "user testing" of my own. Granted, my test wasn't at all scientific and my results weren't statistically significant, but this was the best I could do at the time with minimal resources.

I began walking around the agency to employees who worked in other areas of the company (non-Internet), and were unfamiliar with the project. I asked them to look at the site and to give me their opinions. I didn't tell them why I was asking, other than just to get an opinion and I gave them no instruction, beyond helping them pull up the site on their computers. Out of around a dozen "test subjects,"

The Flash Designer

When designers first began designing web sites, back when Mosaic was the popular browser, expectations for usability weren't discussed. The objective for most designers was getting their Photoshop collage onto the server, and then turning it into a server-side image map. Like all new media, in its infancy it was primitive and sometimes not very user friendly. Some might only one person figured out they needed to click on one of the little moving letters to go anywhere. The others sat there looking dazed and confused, and finally asked me, "Is there anything else? Is it just this one page? What am I supposed to do?" Once I got everyone past the home page, I thought it might get a little better. But it didn't; instead it got worse. Now that people had the idea to move their mouse around to find the "mystery," they started clicking anything that produced a little hand icon. Once they were in two or three pages deep, they tried to return to the home page. No such luck. No Back button and no apparent "home" link (it was there somewhere, just waiting to be found). That was it, they'd had enough. They gave up at that point. I had the "proof" I needed, or so I thought.

I took my findings to the creative director, prepared to win my battle, certain that even a creative director couldn't deny what real users had said. He denied it, and without even an explanation. He told me he liked the design and thought it was cutting edge and we were going to

move forward with it.

It moved forward as far as the client. But, by this time, the entire site had been built. Our client took one stab at trying to figure it out and came back to us demanding we "fix" the navigation. At this point it was too late. A deadline was looming dangerously close and we had no time to redo the whole site.

In the end, the site went live with minor navigation improvements, but with the same basic usability problems it started with. And, it was then I knew what I wanted to do with my life. I wanted to save the world from horribly unusable sites. I wanted to spare unsuspecting users of being taken deep into sites to the point of no return (with no Back button). I wanted to become an information architect.

At the time, I had no idea what was involved in being an information architect, but I did have a pretty good sense for what Internet users wanted and what made a web site usable. To make the rest of this long story much shorter, I was offered a job shortly after the experience I just described with an Internet

development company as an information architect. Since then I have learned a lot, studied a lot, and observed a lot to find out what makes a web site, a software application, or any other interactive medium usable. I've also learned over and over again what I learned from the creative director who pushed me over the edge.

Despite a wealth of usability findings and practical argument, designers will still be designers and "healthy tension" will always exist between designers and information architects. That being said, what I hope to do in this book is provide information, based on my experiences as an information architect and the experiences of others in the field I've learned from, on how to make sure the only tension that exists is the healthy kind. I hope to provide practical examples and solutions to some of the common problems designers and information architects face when it comes to finding a mutual ground between creative design and usability, so the two can coexist (and they can).

–Stephanie Reindel

argue, though, because of the limitations of the browsers, web designers broke less usability rules because they didn't have as many options as we do today. The simplicity of web sites having only HTML links and simple graphics ensured that pages were transmitted easily over slow 2400 baud modems, and that simple browsers could render the pages effectively.

Filter Madness

Anyone who has launched Photoshop for the first time can probably relate to this experience. The first menu item explored is the Filter menu. Through this menu item, the new user begins to see all the wonderful distortions and effects you can apply to a picture with one click of the mouse.

Imagine the design world if all designers simply used filters throughout their work. This would be a world of water-rippled images and glowing edges. Why do we discuss Photoshop when this is a book about Flash usability? Flash has given the web designer more control over every aspect of what makes design good. The quality of typography, color palettes, and image control have all been raised because of the use of Flash. The capability to use embedded fonts alone has raised Flash to godlike status in some design circles. But these new features have come at a price. Just like our Photoshop Filter menu example, Flash has given designers too many options, and with too many options come Flash sites with everything moving and dancing, but with no easy way for a user to navigate through it all. Some Flash sites are so experimental, users must hunt to find the navigation or learn a sequence of mouse clicks to navigate the site.

How the Designer Is Different

The designer interprets the world, problems, and client objectives in a different way than most people on a project development team. The designer has the want—some would even go as far as to say the *need*—to express an inner creative spirit when approaching design. No wonder many Flash sites, when steered strictly by design, end up being the playground for a designer's spirit. Some interface elements in a site can truly confuse users because the designer infused too much of their personality into the navigation, instead of paying homage to the user group for whom the site was intended.

Some high-end design studios have an attitude that "if the user is too stupid to understand the interface, then they should go elsewhere." Unfortunately, this attitude is also prevalent with many Flash designers. Designers naturally rank color, shapes, and typography above information flow, usability, and download time. Designers who spend hours designing an original interface have difficulty going back *after* the design is created and adding elements to enhance usability; for example, adding text labels to a design that's minimalist. Often these types of changes destroy the original design objective when the designer doesn't take usability into account in the original design.

Flash Design Methods

Flash designers start designing their interfaces using several different techniques. Some begin by creating *mood boards* or *concept boards*; these rough-design studies serve as sketches to help the designer interoperate the client's brand identity or main message. Often, these early design comps don't include actual interface elements but, instead, have color swatches, types of typography, photography treatment, and graphic style. Other designers start by collecting magazine images and designs that best fit the client's style. These scraps of paper are pasted onto a large collage board and presented as ways the artist intends to proceed with their graphic treatment of the site. This exercise often doesn't include viewing the styles of how information is laid out (such as text flow or information division) but, rather, is more about how color, type, and photography are treated.

From the initial stage, most Flash designers are thinking about typography and graphic design instead of information flow and usability. Some will argue that design and information flow cannot be separated, and that graphic design is about displaying information. Even if the information is photography, ultimately designers are displaying some type of information, regardless if it's more than the traditional navigation bar. Designers manage complex information using visual communication, but most designers don't willfully sit down to plan a strategy for how information can flow more freely through their Flash site. Much has been written about how designers are sculpting information and how this information is displayed through graphic design. Most designers don't interpret their design this way. For most, design is a natural extension of their personality. It flows from their creative thoughts and, thus, is not perceived as information management but, instead, simply as design.

Many Flash designers in ad agencies, small studios, and multimedia shops jump right into design without doing a little research up front. This is often because they think they know the intended user group or they have what appears to be a clear directive from the client. Try to squeeze some up-front research about the intended user group into the project, even if time and budget don't permit this. *A user group* is a fancy term for the folks who are going to use your site. You can obtain information about your user group simply by quizzing your client for more information about who they think the intended audience is. This is often effective because the client has usually done their own market research for their target audience. If this information isn't available, though, you can do simple sampling by calling people you know who might fit the target audience and asking them questions about how they would use such a Flash site. We go into more detail about user groups and how they function in Chapter 3.

After you get an idea of the target audience, write down who the audience is and, if you have time, find a picture for several users and give them names, hobbies, and interests. Now print that information and leave it beside your computer as you design. You can inject this into your design process. How would this target audience perceive my design? Would this audience understand the flow of information? What style of typography would most appeal to a teenager? Is the latest MTV video font going to make it easier for the teen to accept the brand message? These are all questions that will slowly enter your mind as you design because you have put a face on a person you're designing for—it's not an empty void, it's a person. I believe that by connecting to these people, you can have a greater appreciation for wanting to develop a Flash site they can use, and you can make it a well-designed and interesting place to visit. You have humanized the reason to design a usable site because you're thinking about the real people who will use it.

Clients ask for Flash because they know it helps make their projects more engaging and the sites "stickier." The real world is a different place from the arguments and theoretical debates of information design. Most web development agencies around the world are now creating Flash sites as standard practice for most of their clients. Ad agencies either have in-house expertise in Flash or have close vendor relationships with firms who specialize only in Flash. Because this infrastructure is developed, Flash is now used in most web sites, even if it's limited to small areas of a totally HTML-driven site.

Flash offers both the usability world and the design world so much. Now, thanks to Flash, you can control typography in a way you never could with static HTML. You can make type larger and more readable by embedding highly usable fonts into the Flash file. Custom fonts help deliver the brand message of the site, while ensuring that every end user will see the same font correctly. Problems with the way traditional HTML displayed type made ensuring a common user experience across all platforms difficult for web designers. Fonts would look smaller on Macintosh systems and larger on Windows systems.

Problems such as these have been resolved by the use of Flash. Flash delivered what Java promised but didn't deliver—platform independence— and has begun to show itself as more than just a tool for animation and eye candy. Flash not only has resolved many typography issues, it has resolved functionality problems associated with different browsers and operating systems (OSs). Even simple HTML pages will render differently, depending on what browser you open the page in. Flash renders the layout of SWF files (the file format used by Flash to deliver graphics, animation, and sound over the Internet) the same, regardless of the browser or the OS you're using.

Let's review practices to incorporate into your design that can help get you thinking about usability from the start of the project.

> ❱ Gather as much information about the user group as you can.

> ❱ Create "mock" user profiles and leave them in front of you as you begin your initial designs. Try to imagine what type of interface this user group would be comfortable with.

> ❱ Explore other Flash sites. Imagine the sites from the point of view of a novice computer user. Would the site be easy to navigate? Is the navigation well labeled or does it have a good help system?

Flash offers the designer incredible control over the typography, color, and layout of a site. Flash gives the web designer the capability to lay out a page and ensure it renders the same, regardless of OS or browser. Ultimately, this helps usability because the Flash developer can be assured the layout of the page won't fluctuate between browsers. For people developing large-scale sites, with a diverse user group, maintaining design control is critical to a successful Flash site.

The "Mother Test"

If you can't test your site on your target audience, then try to run tests on users you have on hand. I always like to have my mother sit down in front of what I've designed and see if she can navigate through it easily. My mother is an average computer user; she knows how to log in unattended and check her Hotmail. But she doesn't use the computer every day, so she's a good test user to see if a complex Flash interface will pass the general user test. You can find people like this in your life to help test your Flash projects. Flash designers often overlook an obvious usability flaw—sometimes we can't see the forest for the trees.   –K.A.

K.I.S.S.

K.I.S.S. or Keep It Simple Stupid is an easy acronym, but a helpful one. The raging debates and the intellectual discussions are about what design is and isn't, and how designers are actually high-level, information-management junkies. The simple truth is, however, that most designers do not perceive themselves in this way. They design because it's fulfilling and *fun*.

Thinking about information architecture is foreign to most designers. Design is about limitless boundaries, self-expression, and the possible. Most designers perceive information architecture as setting limits, boundaries, and controls. So, the two disciplines are in opposition to each other— this is the nature of the beast. Flash designers can train themselves to see information architecture in the structures they design; however, this takes some practice and patience. When a Flash designer starts an initial exploration using sketches, concept boards, and so forth, this is a good time to begin thinking about information layout.

Evaluate how other Flash sites use color, typography, and design styles to enhance the information. Notice how other Flash sites use open white spaces to draw your eye to type or how a Flash site crowds the text into a small scrolling box, with small, hard-to-read type. You can learn from both bad and good examples. Although it's inherently difficult for Flash designers to think about information architecture as they design, new steps can be built in to the design process to ensure Flash usability is in place.

Personal Viewpoint
Flash Design from the Agency

Having worked in a large ad agency, I know firsthand the pitfalls many Flash developers run into while trying to develop useable Flash sites. Unfortunately, many ad agencies don't understand information architecture—they simply aren't set up for this. Ad agencies typically are about design and advertising, not about building usable information systems. A Flash web site could be looked at as a simplified computer program. After all, you're designing an interface that's interactive, and many Flash features let developers build complex systems that behave like software, such as Windows, Photoshop, and so forth. So, it's no surprise ad agencies are creating Flash sites that aren't terribly usable because, in fact, they're

applying design to something much more complex than a billboard, magazine ad, or a 30-second commercial. Now, I don't want to give people the wrong impression: some ad agencies are doing a great job at producing usable Flash sites, but this is the exception. I suspect these agencies are using some form of information architecture. This comes back to my original discussion that creative minds in their natural state cannot apply information architecture. It's against our grain to limit our abilities by some set of "design rules." Because of this, many creative departments at ad agencies have directors pushing Flash design with little regard for usability. I don't believe they're pushing design over usability intentionally, but it's their natural

sense that design is what helps sell.

The fearless design leaders at ad agencies are dealing with something totally different from the print ads they worked on originally. And Flash is even a different monster from the static HTML pages these design leaders worked on two years ago. Now, the creative director is dealing with motion, complex interactivity, and connection to back-end database systems. High-end Flash sites are starting to resemble traditional software more and more, so it's no wonder creative directors are having trouble producing usable Flash sites. Creative directors haven't had to think about building complex systems in the past, so they have a high rate of failure when they try to build such systems now.

–Kevin Airgid

Summary

The reality is that designers and information architects need each other. Both bring important assets to the table. Designers bring the creative ingenuity necessary to create interesting, interactive, engaging web site experiences. Information architects bring the usability expertise necessary to ensure that users are able to accomplish their goals at the site without difficulty. Both aspects are necessary in creating a positive user experience. The healthy tension that often exists between the two disciplines is just that—healthy. Without the back and forth, the yin and yang, a site would end up either so jam-packed with creativity that not even the designer could figure out how to use it, or so boring that users would fall asleep before achieving their goals. When taken to the extreme, neither is desirable. The point of this book is to help you understand how and why creative design (particularly design that uses Flash) and usability standards can coexist and *must* coexist for either to be truly successful.

In the next chapter, we look more closely at the pros and cons of focusing strictly on Flash design or on information architecture when developing a site.

Flash Usability Fast Facts

> Usability can be defined as "the extent to which a product can be used by specified users to achieve specified goals with effectiveness, efficiency, and satisfaction in a specified context of use" (ISO 9241–11).

> It is estimated that failure to provide useful content and functionality results in a loss of roughly 40 percent of repeat visitors and 50 percent of lost online sales.

> Usability is achieved by understanding the people who will have the experience, identifying the goals they're trying to accomplish, and uniting them within an engaging design.

> Design elements should be used to add value, enhance functionality, and/or help users accomplish their goals.

> An Information architect's number-one concern is to make sure the product being developed (web site, software application, CD/DVD-ROM, and so forth) fulfills the needs and goals of the target user

group and, at the same time, is easy and intuitive for that group to use.

❯ Remember, your users might have limitations that prevent or hinder their ability to use various Flash elements because of low-grade equipment, slow Internet connections, software deficiencies, or lack of knowledge.

❯ Flash renders a page layout much more consistently than other technologies.

❯ Flash files enable users to use custom fonts to ensure quality graphic design and legibility, regardless of the end user system.

chapter **2**

Design and Usability: The Pros and Cons

As we mentioned in Chapter 1, design and usability go hand in hand. Creating a product that focuses on one, while ignoring the other, detracts from the overall user experience. Flash is a powerful design tool that, when used wisely, can exploit visual appeal and at the same time enhance usability. Usability standards play an indispensable role in helping users achieve their goals and come away with a positive impression. Design and usability, however, are not without weaknesses when used in the absence of good judgment and accurate background information. In this chapter, we explore some of the pros and cons of using Flash, as well as the pros and cons of incorporating usability standards. In doing so, we hope to help you understand the importance of incorporating the right mix of usability and design to achieve optimum results.

Pros and Cons of Designing with Flash

In the field of usability, you won't read too many lines of text written about the pros of using Flash. A long list of cons exists, but few examples of good practices are available. Many leading information architects have demonized Flash for being unusable, but none of these experts has come forward with solutions. Pointing a finger and finding fault is easy, but finding viable solutions isn't. Most information architects have a background in computer interface design, library and information sciences, or large-scale web site development. Not many information architects come from multimedia backgrounds or have experience with motion and interactive solutions. No wonder then that all the information architects can do is point out the problems. Providing viable solutions is well beyond their experience. This is why the Flash developer must do double duty. Flash developers not only must be aware of design, motion, and interactivity, they must also become sensitive to usability issues to deliver successful Flash sites. This is a lot to ask for a group of people already working many extra hours to meet the demanding schedules of Internet time. But, it's essential for Flash developers to take an active role in ensuring a usable Flash site because many other professionals in the field are unable to bring solutions to the table.

Flash designers can take a more active role in creating usable Flash sites by doing a little research up front. By knowing your target audience, you can define a standard objective for a Flash site. As we mentioned in the previous chapter, writing down and becoming familiar with your user group (or target audience) is important before you start designing a Flash interface. Before you begin designing a Flash interface, follow these steps:

> ❭ Ask your client questions. Who does your client think is the user audience? Has your client done any previous research?

> ❭ If your client hasn't done research, try to have some research funds added to the budget. If the budget doesn't allow for research, do some quick user profile studies of your own. Estimating a target audience, and then discussing this with your client, can shed new light on your project goals.

> ❭ Create user profiles. Give each user a name, an age, and a short biography to profile how a potential user can approach your Flash site.

> ❭ Define the primary goals of the site.

> ❭ Determine who are the primary and secondary audiences.

> ❭ Decide the audience capabilities regarding browser, connection speed, and computer speed.

Flash is not perfect. We hope by providing both positive and negative aspects of Flash we can help illustrate how to avoid the pitfalls many Flash developers encounter with the program. By demonstrating with best-case and worst-case scenarios, we hope to educate you on the path to a usable Flash site.

Flash Pros

Flash has many benefits. The user can be given more control over printing and can review streaming elements before the file downloads, to remove the awareness of the download delay. Designers benefit from the pixel-precise control to lay out large amounts of images and text.

Printing in Flash Is Better for Graphics

Because Flash uses vector technology, it offers web developers a whole new frontier that would never have been realized without its distribution. Because Flash files can contain simple vector objects that include mathematical statements on how to draw images, developers can dynamically change the images located in the Flash movie. The capability to change the content dynamically enables Flash developers to prepare a piece of Flash content for whatever the requirements of the end users. We'll use a real-world example to demonstrate how Flash can be used to enhance web printing. Imagine we're creating a Flash site for a company that builds swing sets. These swing sets are complicated to assemble and have many parts. As with all products, the swing set comes with a black-and-white set of instructions because providing color instructions is too costly.

The manufacturer of the swing sets has done some user research and learned the customer base would be interested in having more detailed assembly instructions online. The manufacturer develops a Flash site that enables the users to view the assembly instructions from all angles. When the user finds the swing set instructions and diagrams required, they press a smart print button in the Flash movie. The Flash movie then presents the user with several print options for the file: in full color, in gray scale, or as a line drawing. Flash could remove detail on the diagram on-the-fly, based on the user's hardware capabililities. This would enable users with lower-end printers to print simple, line art instructions, and users with new bubble-jet printers to print more detailed color instructions.

This type of printing solution typically couldn't be offered by a traditional web site. To supply this printing functionality to the end user without Flash, the site would have to be database-driven and graphics would have to be dynamically generated on demand. This would add a tremendous load to the server if the site received many user sessions. By using Flash, the developer downloads processing requirements to the client. Because Flash is a vector format, the resulting printout will match the user's printer and print the best possible image, unlike static low-resolution GIF or JPEG files.

Smart Flash Navigation

One of the biggest complaints about Flash is that developers "break" the Back button in the browser. We cover this issue more in Chapter 4, but Flash can be programmed to create a Back button that not only enables the user to go backward in a web site, but allows the user to go back in an animation sequence or in layered image sequence. Don't try that with your average web page! Creating navigation in Flash is flexible, but this flexibility

Personal Viewpoint
Flash Printing of Company News

When I first began building our company Flash web site, shown here, it was important that the news on the home page was easy to update. Our programming department built a PHP back end that enabled users to enter a secure administration area to update the news section online. This PHP application was then called on by the Flash movie to populate the text areas of the news area. Once the text was loaded into the Flash movie using PHP, it was displayed in an easy-to-read format for the Web. This format was suitable for reviewing the text on the end user monitor, but it didn't meet the requirements our writer wanted for a proper news release.

Using an ActionScript and with a little help from Macromedia's Printing SDK (which you can find by searching for Flash Printing SDK in the Macromedia Flash Support Area at http://www.macromedia.com/support/flash/), I created a second symbol that reformatted the imported text. I made the text larger, changed the layout to match a standard press release, and formatted it to print to a full 8½ by 11 sheet of paper. By doing this, I was able to retain the pleasing web presentation and enable the user to print a "printer friendly" version without the need for our programming department to build some type of complex back-end system to reformat an HTML page. Also, this Flash printing enabled the user instant access to print the document without having to wait several more seconds for the server to generate a new version for printing, and then force the browser to download a whole new version that's more suitable for printing. The information was already contained in the Flash movie the user downloaded. All I did was use Flash's ActionScript to reformat the text.

–Kevin Airgid

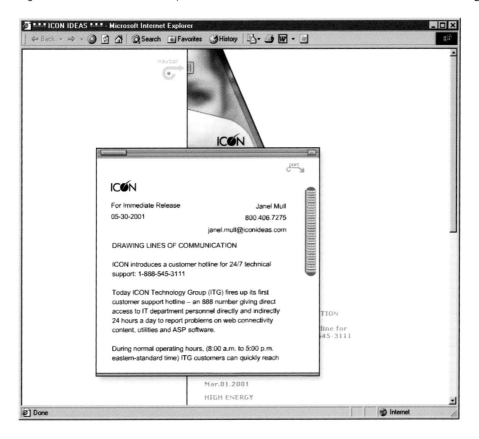

shouldn't interfere with the usability of a site. Just because you have an unlimited set of tools at your disposal doesn't mean you should use them. Sticking to interface elements the user is comfortable with is important. For most user groups, standard graphic user interface controls should be employed. This means creating scroll bars, windows, and other widgets that behave like the standard interface controls the users are familiar with on their operating systems (OSs). That being said, you can use Flash to enhance these interface elements to make the site even more usable and aesthetically pleasing.

By using ActionScript, you can detect the speed of the user's Internet connection. With this information, the developer can instruct the Flash movie to load the appropriate content. If the user is surfing with a dial-up connection, the Flash movie could be instructed to load a low-bandwidth version of the site. If the user's bandwidth is DSL, cable, or some other broadband connection, the Flash movie could serve up a broadband version of the navigation. The broadband version of the navigation could contain more bitmap images or more complex vector drawings. The dial-up version of the navigation could be outlines or simple text in boxes to ensure a fast download.

With traditional HTML web sites, users are typically stuck with the navigation regardless of their connection. Flash navigation can also be dynamically created for other reasons. The navigation could provide the capability to increase in size on the screen. This would enable users with disabilities, such as poor vision, to view detailed site navigation with greater detail. One of the complaints about Flash is its lack of accessibility for disabled persons. (For more on addressing usability for people with disabilities, see Chapter 6.) Because Flash content can be fluid and dynamic, Flash ActionScript can be used to scale objects within the movie that people need to look at with greater detail. Navigation could be scaled with a simple button labeled Enlarge Navigation. Once again, traditional web sites built in HTML are unable to offer this type of functionality. (Most OSs offer accessibility functionality, such as a screen magnifier, but this isn't always enabled, especially for people using public computers at libraries and Internet cafés.) People who wear glasses often find reading text onscreen difficult. By offering users the capability to increase the font size through Flash ActionScript, you increase the usability of your site for a wider range of viewers.

The ActionScript required to implement scaling navigation, text, and other symbols is relatively easy. You can obtain example movies at Flash developer portals, such as The Flash Kit (http://www.flashkit.com/).

Animation Is Best in Flash

Flash has its roots as an animation tool. Because Flash uses vector technology to draw elements on the screen, the file sizes are small. Once downloaded on the client browser, the client CPU uses the math to draw the animation in real time on the computer. The task of rendering the images is downloaded to the end user's computer. Using ActionScript, the Flash developer can detect how fast the user's computer can draw the animation. ActionScript routines can enable developers to calculate how many frames per second a given computer is capable of drawing. Using this information, the developer can gear the animation sequence to the user's computer.

The Flash developer could build a Flash movie that reduces the detail of the animation sequence to have the sequence play faster on slower computers. This would be impossible to do automatically using any format other than Flash for animation. If the end user has a fast CPU and graphics card, the Flash developer could increase the size of the movie window, so the user could enjoy a more cinematic experience online. The capability for Flash to scale and tween gives its animation limitless possibilities. Flash animators can scale the same object from small to large without needing to download in-between frames, such as an animated GIF or digital video file. Flash can tween (or calculate the in-between) sequences on-the-fly as the movie draws on the user's computer.

ActionScript can be used to animate objects on the stage with much more control than languages such as JavaScript or DHTML. Because ActionScript is executed on every computer the same way, Flash developers can apply real-time effects to symbols on the stage with no worry that the Action Script won't be compatible between platforms. For instance, a Flash developer could create an ActionScript that would change the X and Y scale of a symbol on the stage dynamically. This ActionScript would make the symbol appear to look like silly putty being stretched quickly. The ActionScript would then function properly on any browser or OS that had the proper Flash player.

Animation in Flash can consume less bandwidth because Flash animators can reuse symbols (or graphic images) over and over. The same symbol can be used multiple times on the stage to create a complex-looking animation. The Flash movie only needs to download one source for the data, and then the Flash player replicates the image by using the processing power of the end user's computer system.

Layout Control: Freaks in Heaven!

One of the greatest benefits of developing a site in Flash is the total control of the layout of the page. When a Flash designer places an image 10 pixels from the top and 80 pixels from the left, this is where the image will appear in every Flash player that reads the movie. DHTML, cascading style sheets (CSS), and even simple HTML are all at the mercy of a browser's rendering engine. Anyone who has tried to get a complex layout—created using nested tables, CSS, and DHTML—has run into the Netscape versus Internet Explorer crunch. When coding HTML pages using these technologies, the developer becomes painfully aware of how buggy and different each browser renders the page layout.

Imagine if you were working in an environment where your user group used Macintosh, Windows 95, 98, and XP. Every OS shipped with a different browser and each browser would render the pages differently. Developers often have to write subroutines and workarounds to get all the code to work on all browsers. By using Flash, all these issues disappear. Because Flash is controlled by one company, it's more reliable and stable than many of the HTML standards. A Flash designer can be assured that when a form is created, the shape, color, and exact position on the page can be controlled, down to the pixel. This reduces development time and increases usability across a wide user group.

Flash offers developers the capability to embed fonts into the Flash file. This feature ensures that a Flash movie can contain proper typography that will help to promote an organization's brand message. Typography is one of the key factors of good design. Until recently, designers were forced to use bitmap images to transmit unique fonts in their design. In doing so, they disabled the capability for users to select the type and reduced the legibility of the type when it was printed. Flash can transmit the custom font in vector format, so the characters can be selected for copying and easily printed in a sharp, crisp format.

International character sets can also be embedded in Flash files. This means users can transmit other languages using Flash to computer users who might not have the language set installed on their computers. A good example would be someone using a computer in a library, an airport, or an Internet café where English is the only character system in use. In this age of globalization, users might speak English as their second language, so it's important for some sites to offer multiple languages. Flash can serve up another language without the need to install a new character set.

Flash can streamline production of low-bandwidth sites. Flash has a unique capability to load information on layers, much the same way Photoshop has layers. Each layer can contain a separate movie loaded from an external source. These layers can be controlled and moved from within the parent movie. This capability to load layers makes Flash an excellent choice for developing low-bandwidth sites because developers can load parts of a site on a need-to-have basis. Flash also offers excellent streaming capabilities. Once the developer researches and uses the streaming capabilities more effectively, the developer can gradually load movie content without the user realizing they're waiting for content. A good example is to turn off the "loading" movie message you see in so many Flash movies and provide text trivia in the browser window while the content loads in the background. This is illustrated in Amnesty International's 40th Anniversary Flash movie (see Figure 2-1), which uses streaming techniques to occupy the user while the movie downloads.

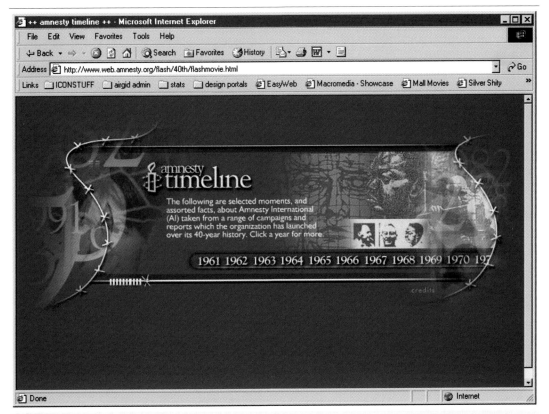

FIGURE 2-1

Amnesty International's 40th Anniversary Flash movie streams content while the movie downloads (copyright 2001 Amnesty International)

Personal Viewpoint
Using Layers

While building my portfolio Flash site, shown here, I became aware of the need to have two separate sites. One site needed to be geared to low-bandwidth users and the other to broadband users. My target audience was creative directors and multimedia companies (I was looking for work at the time).

So I built a design-oriented site, but the site needed to work well at 56K and on DSL or cable modems. I found many creative directors— especially at large agencies—didn't have a lot of office time to look at the portfolios of potential new hires. Consequently, they would go home and use their 56K connection to review the work. So, I had to make a site that functioned well at high and low bandwidths. I didn't have time to create separate sites, so I used Flash's capability to load movies on separate layers to help remove the fluff from the low-bandwidth version. In the low-bandwidth version, I simply removed one line of ActionScript that loaded the music for the site. This reduced the file download by 1MB! My final file was well within the comfortable range of 56K, so I streamed in the layers without the need for a long delay with a "loading" message.

–Kevin Airgid

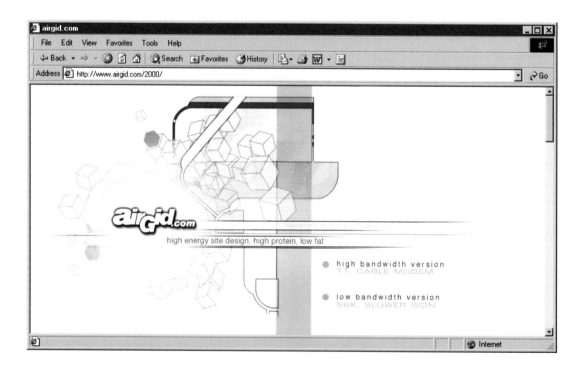

Flash Cons

There are many cons when using Flash, so it is important to be aware of them as you proceed to build a usable Flash site. By knowing the limitations of the software, you can learn to avoid the mistakes many Flash developers initially make.

Bitmap Images Don't Load Well in Flash

Flash, for all its capability to save designers from boring fonts such as Verdana, Arial, and Times Roman, has several drawbacks for graphic design. By working with these drawbacks instead of against them, Flash developers can hope to achieve more usable sites. At its core, Flash is an interactive tool for vector files. Flash does handle bitmap files, but it doesn't have some of the benefits of using bitmap files in ordinary HTML. Because Flash files are compiled, the bitmap images are grouped in with other parts of the Flash file and aren't transmitted separately as with HTML pages. When HTML pages load, the browser begins to read the code from the top of the page, and then loads the pictures individually.

The browser begins to stream in the pictures, so the user can begin to view the pictures before they're totally downloaded. This enables the user to begin reviewing the document before it's loaded and eliminates the feeling of waiting most users experience with Flash. Flash developers can stream parts of the Flash movie into the browser, but Flash has no way to show a partially downloaded image. The user must wait until the bitmap image is completely downloaded to view it. This impacts graphic design because if a designer has a rich Photoshop collage she wants to use in a Flash movie, she must find creative ways to occupy the user while it loads.

Flash Version Problems

Although Flash has a high rate of penetration in the browser market, many developers fail to consider that Flash 3 and Flash 4 are the most prevalent plug-ins. Forcing users to upgrade to Flash 5 so the Flash developer can use Flash 5 features might reduce how many people enter your site. Many of the new scripting features of Flash 5 make it a must-have for developers, but are you paying a price for these new features by driving away potential customers? Macromedia offers an Active-X control update (for Windows users) online, but many companies and IT departments have locked down the installation of Active-X controls. This means your users might not be able or might not know how to upgrade from Flash 4 to the Flash 5 player. Macromedia offers many excellent ActionScripts and JavaScripts to help detect for the correct version of Flash. To learn more, visit the Macromedia Flash support center at http://www.macromedia.com/support/flash/.

My Wheel Mouse Is Broken!

One of the features many web designers are employing in design portal sites is iframes, an Internet Explorer–specific way of placing a scrolling area on a screen without having to scroll the whole page. This new HTML feature offers the capability to place more content on a page without using hard-to-manage frames. It is much like the scrolling areas many Flash developers create to house copious amounts of images or text. The drawback to using Flash for scrolling objects and text is that the wheel mouse is rendered useless. After surfing for hours with a wheel mouse, many users find it difficult to come to a site that eliminates this easy-to-use invention. Unfortunately, no way exists to resolve this issue in the current release of Flash.

Two Steps Forward, One Step Back

One of the drawbacks of designing in Flash is you have to create interface elements continuously. Simple form objects, such as drop-down menus, radio buttons, checkboxes, scroll bars, menus, and basic Submit buttons, all must be created from scratch in Flash. Macromedia does offer some prebuilt templates of these objects, but they're hardly a standard like the interface objects created by the browser. Because no standard way exists to generate interface objects in Flash, users are forced to create custom interface elements.

One of the reasons Flash developers have broken many usability roles is because Flash often forces designers to render GUI elements using their own sets of tools. You can often tell what type of system Flash designers have created their custom GUI elements from: Macintosh users often include Mac OS–looking scroll bars, which look foreign to Windows users, and vice versa. At least HTML pages render scroll bars, form elements, and other interface elements in the same style as the OS and browser the user is using. This way, all forms on the Web have something in common. Unfortunately, although this creative freedom enables Flash designers to increase the design control, it also makes using common interface elements a challenge for some users.

Flash Considerations

Although Flash offers flexibility, it also presents usability challenges in the areas of interface design and interface standards. Flash developers must ask if Flash adds value to a project. Then they must pursue how to use Flash effectively to meet the needs and goals of their target audience.

When Is It Better to Use Digital Video?

Streaming video offers the closest to cinematic experience the Web can produce. It's an extremely rich media, too rich in fact for most lowly dial-up connections. So, is it any wonder that Flash has exploded because it can display this larger animation on the screen? Streaming video is excellent for relaying information presented in real time, such as small news clips where live video can tell a story more effectively than text or a hard-to-produce animation. Streaming video is best suited for events that would take too long or be too costly to create in Flash animation. The other reason to use digital video is when you want to produce highly layered bitmap effects in programs such as Adobe After Effects or Apple's iMovie. Here's a list of good uses of streaming video:

- ❭ Movie trailers
- ❭ Samples of a video that might be for sale on an e-commerce site
- ❭ Distribution media for a movie "short" created by a low-budget team or an individual artist
- ❭ Short home movies for relatives around the world with broadband connection
- ❭ Converting training videos to digital video to be reviewed by employees across an intranet
- ❭ Live events, such as keynote speeches by top executives

When Is It Better to Use an HTML-Driven Site?

HTML versus Flash has been a hot topic for many Flash developers. A backlash to the use of Flash on sites has occurred because of the gratuitous use of intro animations and eye candy. Flash has its place but, once again, you must assess your user audience. When should you use Flash? Research your user audience. Will animation, interactivity, and the other features Flash offers add value to your site? Or, will these things get in the way of delivering the main message to your target audience? HTML sites will function well for low-end users. Does your target audience use extremely slow computers? If so, you might want to use an HTML site because simple HTML and graphics can be displayed on the most modest of computer monitors. Is your target audience young males between the ages of 20 and 30? Then you can use interactivity and animation if it helps add value to your message.

Ask Yourself: Does Flash Add Value?

This is the question you need to ask yourself, regardless of your target audience. Even if your audience is capable of viewing Flash and has a robust computer system, it still might not value or want Flash in the site. Many people confuse the technical level of the target audience with its goal-seeking objectives. The target audience might have a cable modem and a fast CPU and graphics card, but all it might require from your site is the capability to download text. What good will Flash be to these users if you force them to review eye-candy intro animations, regardless of whether it downloads fast. What's the objective when a user enters the site?

Pros and Cons of Designing for Usability

You might wonder why we even spend time discussing something as obvious as the benefits of usability. After all, it seems only logical that designers, clients, and users would agree a product should be usable. And what's that in the title about "cons" of usability? It would seem, after all the evangelizing we've heard from the hardcore usability experts of the world, a downside to usability couldn't possibly exist. Much confusion still occurs when it comes to recognizing the most beneficial aspects of usability principles, as well as the potential problems they can create. Both designers and information architects must understand how usability principles can work for and against the overall user experience to defend usability effectively.

Personal Viewpoint
Building a Web Site Is Like Writing a Good Essay

I've always thought that building a good web site is like writing a good essay. I had an English teacher in high school who made us stick to a strict formula for writing essays to help us become better writers. This formula involved writing an opening thesis argument, and then providing three clear statements that presented evidence the argument was true. Developing a web site is much like this method of essay writing. You must find out what the main objective of your site is, and then provide clear paths to fulfill this objective. This means using tools and technology that properly address the objective with creative solutions.

–Kevin Airgid

Usability Pros

Generally, we all begin the design process with good intentions for usability. Imagining a designer who set out to create a site that was intentionally frustrating, confusing, uninviting, and unusable would be difficult. However, even the most well-intentioned designers sometimes lose sight of usability issues in the midst of the creative process. Compared with the opportunity to incorporate and, perhaps, even show off the coolest, most innovative Flash technology, suddenly usability doesn't seem so important. When it comes to overlooking usability, clients are also guilty. Many clients lose sight of usability when they're presented with a budget and realize that incorporating good usability isn't cheap. Early in a project, it is all too easy for clients to scratch off the proposal the time and money required to develop a user-centric design. When put to the final test, though, the consequences of neglecting the user are apparent, to the detriment of everyone involved. For these reasons, it's important that we take the time to better understand the benefits of incorporating usability principles early on, before it's too late.

Usability Benefits the User

Sites that reflect the needs and desires of their key user groups in both form and function provide those users with an overall positive experience—one that enables them to do what they came to the site to do, and to do it efficiently, effectively, and with satisfaction. Smiles are a little wider, blood pressures are a little lower, interests are peaked, and confidence in what is still, to many, an unfamiliar and uncertain medium climbs a notch.

Good usability should be virtually invisible to users. When a site is easy to use, users won't even think about how they're using it or what they can or can't figure out how to do. Instead they're allowed to focus their attention on the content, the design, and the brand message being conveyed. All the time and effort you spent creating that cool Flash content won't be wasted because the user is too preoccupied with trying to navigate, turn off the sound, or skip the long download to notice it. Goals will be achieved, products purchased, information found, aesthetics enjoyed, errors (both system and user errors) minimized, productivity increased, and trust and confidence built. And, best of all, users will return.

Thirsting for Usability

Another way to look at the benefits of usability is to consider the problems and frustrations that arise when usability is ignored. Imagine yourself as a user. It's a hot summer day and you want to purchase a soda from a vending machine outside a local retail store. You notice the old machine has been replaced with a new, more modern one. This is much cooler than those old boring machines you remember—there's even a video playing on the front and music in the background. You walk up and start to look around on the machine to find out how much change you need to drop in to get your soda, but the price is nowhere to be found. After a minute or two of searching, you notice a small .75 in the top-right corner. You assume this must be the price and you dig into your pocket for some change. You come out with two quarters and three dimes. "Close enough," you think to yourself, "it will make change." You look around again on the front of the machine for a coin slot to deposit your money into, but this is nowhere to be found. You start feeling around on the front of the machine for a familiar, small, rectangular groove, but still you find no sign of a coin slot. Just as you're about to give up and go across the street to one of those good old-fashioned machines, you see what looks like an indentation on the side of the machine. On further inspection, you determine this must be where you put the change. You drop in the quarters first—one, two. Next come the three dimes. The machine replies back in a loud, intrusive voice: "Incorrect Change. Please Try Again." Your dimes fall out of the bottom of the machine and roll across the sidewalk. You manage to pick up two of them and fumble around in your pockets for more change. Ah-ha—a nickel, just what you need. You drop the two dimes and the nickel in and get ready to select your beverage, but not before you hear that loud voice again: "Quarters Only. Please Try Again." Again, your rejected change falls to the ground.

Feeling determined at this point, you fumble through your pockets one last time in search of a quarter and deep in the corner of your back pocket you find one. At last! Feeling pretty thirsty at this point, you drop in your final quarter and get ready to choose your soda. But wait ... you can see some cool-looking product logos and designs on the front of the machine, but you don't see any buttons to push. You're getting frantic now and start pushing everything that looks like it even resembles a selection button. Finally, you hear that old familiar clank, clank, clank of the can. You look around the machine—on the front, on the side, and finally on the back you spot a small black trapdoor. You push it open to pull out your soda only to find the machine has given you the wrong kind. You shout a few short obscenities at the machine, give it a kick, and go across the street. At least there you know how to get what you want.

If this machine had incorporated some usability standards along with the cool new design to make the purchase process more intuitive, you would've known immediately where to put in your money and how to select your beverage, and you would've walked away a happy, thirst-

quenched customer. You might even have remembered some of the cool features you
encountered, like the video, the music, and how it talked. And, who knows, you might have been
so impressed with the new machine that you'd have gone home and told your friends and family
about it. You probably wouldn't even remember how easy it was to buy the soda (you didn't
expect it to be difficult to begin with), you'd only remember that, overall, it was a cool,
interesting soda purchasing experience. Okay, that might be a bit of an overdramatization—
after all, it is only a soda. But when the experience involves your time, your energy, and your
money it might not seem so trivial.

Usability Benefits the Client

Clients sometimes have a more difficult time recognizing the benefits of
ensuring the usability of their products. This might sound a little ridiculous
because it seems anyone who spends the time and money to create a
product would want people to be able to use it. The problem is this:
when budgets are shrinking and timelines are tight, the time and money
associated with ensuring usability can be eliminated all too easily. Many
clients assume the only real necessities for creating a site are the people
who design it and the people who build it and/or make it work. To these
clients, everything else is dispensable.

This theory might work fine for getting a site up quickly and with minimal
cost, but it doesn't do anything to ensure the success of the site. As we've
already mentioned, success depends greatly on the way people who use the
site perceive their experience. If no one can use the site and, therefore, no
one comes to it or purchases from it, then regardless of how much money
was saved by ignoring usability, everything spent was spent in vain. In the
end, additional time and money will be spent to revamp the site to improve
user satisfaction, and often more will be spent than would've been required
to do the job right the first time.

In comparison, when a client does put forth the resources necessary to
ensure a usable product, the benefits are enormous. Development costs are
actually lower in the end because of fewer revisions both during and after
development. Because user errors will be reduced and frustration minimized,
more users can complete their goals on the site and perceive a positive
experience. A positive experience for the user translates into benefits for the
client, including a positive brand image, increased sales (for e-commerce
sites), a competitive advantage over competitors with less usable sites,
and a greater chance the customer will recommend the site to others.

Also important to remember is clients hire designers and development
companies to create products and sites for them because they lack the
experience and expertise to do so effectively themselves. Because a client is

paying for the expertise of the designer, the information architect, and the rest of the team, it would seem the client would be willing to accept expert advice when provided. This isn't always the case, however. You've probably experienced clients who seemed to believe they knew more about the design and architecture of the site than the "experts" they hired to develop it.

For some clients, the only thing they know about Flash is it's the latest buzzword and their number-one competitor is using it. This might not sound like much, but it's enough to bring clients to the conclusion that they, too, must use Flash. They might not know where, how, or why. They might not even know what Flash does. They just know they want it. As the expert, this is where you must use your knowledge of Flash and usability standards to help clients understand how and why they should incorporate Flash. Not every client will choose to listen and take your advice. Some clients choose to learn the hard way through unhappy users, reduced sales, and, consequently, a poor brand image. If this is the case, then at least you've done your job by advising them correctly.

On the other hand, let's look at what might happen if you fail to provide clients with the necessary advice and direction they might need to help them avoid making potentially fatal mistakes (fatal to their business, that is). Let's say, not wanting to "rock the boat," you go along without objecting to a single request. As a result, your client ends up with a site that incorporates a lengthy loading sequence, an unavoidable Flash introduction, and a complex animated navigation system. Users are frustrated, annoyed, and confused. Many will never return. In the end, who do you think your clients will blame for the usability problems that drove away their customers? Themselves? No way. They'll be pointing their fingers at you—regardless of whether you're legitimately to blame—and they might even question your expertise. On the other hand, if you use your knowledge to help clients understand how to create a site that promotes usability, the resulting user benefits will translate to client benefits, which, most likely, will translate to benefits for those responsible for developing the site in the form of praise, repeat business, and referrals. As you can see, designing for usability benefits everyone involved.

Usability Cons

Believe it or not, on occasion you might come across an instance where usability seems to works against itself. We've mentioned this before and it's worth mentioning again—a truly usable product is one that incorporates the right mix of design and usability to produce the optimal user experience. Usability alone won't achieve the best user experience.

Remember, the user experience is made up of more than just effectiveness and efficiency. The user experience is shaped by other attributes as well, such as aesthetics and the initial impression a user gets when they come to a site for the first time. These attributes are determined to a great degree by the art, graphics, and multimedia design elements the site incorporates.

Some usability activists have insisted—in the name of usability—that web sites incorporate only minimal graphics, default browser fonts and colors, and no plug-ins whatsoever. They've issued a decree on the placement of navigation and dismissed animation altogether. The problem with such a black-and-white perspective is that usability isn't black and white. Usability depends, to a great extent, on users and how they interact with and react to a system. Users come in all shapes and sizes. They have different abilities, limitations, needs, wants, expectations, goals, likes, and dislikes. To say that any one particular usability "rule" could or should be applied in every situation defeats much of the research an information architect performs early in the development process as a means of getting to know target users and their goals. The point of getting to know the users is to understand what can make an interaction experience enjoyable and satisfying to their unique goals and desires. When information architecture is employed as a means of overriding design with uncompromising guidelines, the result is a site that might be usable in terms of functionality, but is unusable in terms of the user experience as a whole. Usability guidelines must be applied within the context of the goals of the site and the audience. Think of usability as the glue that binds together users and content, all against the backdrop of the company's goals.

To illustrate this point further, let's look at two contrasting sites. Figure 2-2 shows a web site used to support the Fourth Web Conference on Human Factors and the Web. As you can see, strict usability guidelines were applied to the design. Navigation is located on the left, links are shown in blue underlined text, and few, if any, graphic elements are present. Does this rather boring interface mean the user experience has been diminished in some way? No, not necessarily. Remember, when assessing usability and the user experience, all contributing factors must be taken into consideration.

The goal of this web site is simple—to provide information to the people within the Human Factors (aka usability/information architecture) community about an upcoming conference. The target user group came to this site with goals and expectations of finding information on where the conference would be located, dates and times of events, instructions on how to register, and other related information. They weren't interested in seeing lots of graphics or images that weren't relevant to their needs or goals. Instead, the group was mainly interested in finding factual information quickly and easily. Additionally, the principal target user group (human factors engineers) was

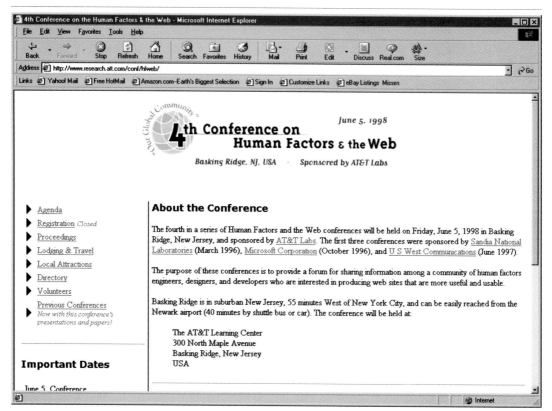

FIGURE 2-2

Fourth web conference on human factors and the Web

composed of people who, because of their profession, are typically familiar and comfortable with this type of simple, easy-to-use interface.

If this same design had been applied to a web site for a company that specialized in design and multimedia development, the story would've been different. Then we could argue that adhering to strict usability guidelines was doing a disservice to the overall user experience. Doing so would've imposed limitations on the incorporation of design and multimedia elements that would have been important for developing the company's brand image. The site shown in Figure 2-3 is a perfect example of this concept. Here's a site that breaks virtually every usability standard in the book. The entire site (with the exception of a PDF version of a resume) uses Flash. Navigation isn't at the top or the left.

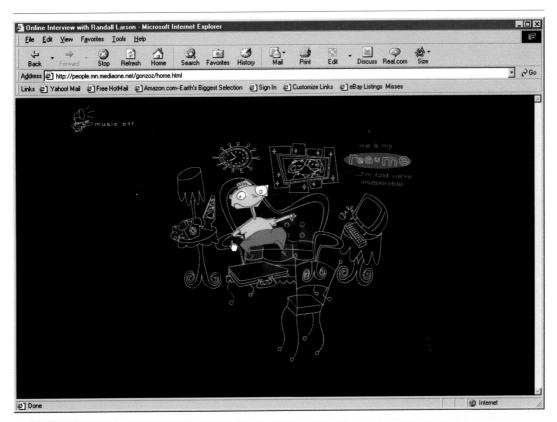

FIGURE 2-3

Online interview with Randall Larson (home page with navigation shown)

In fact, the navigation isn't even visible until you roll your mouse over one of the images. Sound and animation are incorporated throughout and not once will you find a blue underlined link. Even so, this site is extremely usable. Why? Well, to start, the site does incorporate basic usability principles. Content is organized logically. The navigation is logical and relatively easy to learn. Users are kept informed of where they are in the site at all times and can easily go back. The key is these usability principles were applied in the context of the site's goals and the goals, needs, and abilities of the target users. This site represents the personal portfolio of a creative developer.

One of the main goals of the site is obviously to showcase the developer's talents, particularly as they apply to the web design and Flash, to promote and sell his creative design services. Users who would come to a site like this are those familiar with creative design and Flash and are looking for examples of this type of work. These users wouldn't expect to find a list of text links down the left, and they would expect a highly creative and unique experience. Remember, expectations determine, in part, how satisfied a user is with the overall experience. Imagine how users would react if they came to this site expecting to find an example of highly creative design work and, instead, found an interface similar to that of Figure 2-2. The question might then become not could they use it, but would they? Or, would they immediately lose interest and go to a more creative competitor's site? The answer is obvious.

Whether a site is usable depends not only on how functional and well organized it is, but also on how well a site engages its users. In the first example (Figure 2-2), simple, well-organized content and information are exactly what users are looking for and these are enough to keep them engaged. In the second example (Figure 2-3), users are looking for a much more visually stimulating and interactive experience, including examples of Flash design and animation. In both cases, usability standards can and must be applied in a way that enhances the entire user experience.

Summary

In and of themselves, neither Flash nor usability principles alone lead to the optimal user experience. You must consider the strengths and weaknesses of both, and then apply them accordingly within the framework of your project. Flash design and usability practices are tools that, when applied in a vacuum—ignoring relevant goal factors—have a negative effect on the overall experience. When these tools are used together, however, compromising when necessary to support the purpose of the site and the goals of the users, the integrity of the overall experience is reinforced. In the next chapter, we look in depth at the importance of knowing your audience to enhance the user experience with Flash.

Flash Usability Fast Facts

) Flash offers expanded printing capabilities, such as reformatting text for a better printing experience for the end user.

) Stream in parts of your Flash movie so users needn't view long "Loading" messages. This makes your Flash movie appear to be loading faster.

❭ Flash 3 and 4 are the most commonly installed versions of the Flash plug-in. If possible, try to save back to an older version to avoid making people upgrade to a new plug-in.

❭ Use ActionScript to detect which version of the plug-in the browser is running.

❭ If you have extremely long scrolling text, consider placing this information outside Flash, so users can regain control and scroll with their wheel mouse.

❭ Usability guidelines must be applied within the context of the goals of the site and the audience.

❭ Whether a site is usable depends not only on how functional and well organized it is, but also on how well the site engages its users.

❭ Usability guidelines are the glue that binds together users and content, all against the backdrop of the company's goals.

❭ When designing a site, when, where, and how you use Flash should be determined by the purpose of the site and the goals, needs, abilities, and limitations of the users.

> I do think there is merit in challenging the user, but to be intuitive it has to make sense.
>
> –Andries Odendaal,
> Wireframe Studio

chapter

3

Know Your Goal, Know Your Audience

In this chapter, we take a closer look at the importance of understanding your target audience, also known as your users, as well as understanding the goal of the product you're designing. Having a solid understanding of both the audience and end product is essential in determining when, where, and how to incorporate Flash into the design. We explore the factors that affect a user's interactive needs, goals, capabilities, and limitations. We identify key purposes and objectives for various types of products and illustrate how Flash design can either support or obstruct the purpose. The objective is to help you develop the thought process necessary to identify the reason for a product's existence, the characteristics and goals of the people who'll use that product, and how Flash can be used to support both in the design.

What Are Your Goals?

The first step in designing any product is defining the goal of the product. In other words, why are you creating this product? This step is so obvious, it's sometimes overlooked, and yet it's vital to the creative process. Defining the goal (the reason the product exists) can provide the background necessary to begin defining the requirements (what the product must do). The product requirements are further defined by determining the goals of the end users in relation to the product. Defining requirements is important because the requirements, in turn, determine the scope of the project. The scope is defined by the amount of time and work necessary to meet the requirements. When the scope of the project is left undefined because of an unclear site purpose or indistinct users' goals, you can encounter what's known as *feature creep*, which is the tendency for project requirements to snowball out of control because of feature additions and modifications.

Client requests are typically blamed for initiating feature creep; however, a passionate designer's unguided creative energy can also be guilty. A good idea is to evaluate your design in terms of the product goals at each step in the design process to make sure the purpose is being met and your creativity hasn't led you off course. Well-defined goals can also provide an obvious tool for assessing the success of the final product when it's complete.

Types of Goals

The main goal of most web sites probably falls into at least one of the following categories:

> ❭ Provide information
>
> ❭ Provide a service
>
> ❭ Generate revenue
>
> ❭ Provide education or training
>
> ❭ Promote a company or product
>
> ❭ Provide entertainment
>
> ❭ Provide a portal

It isn't uncommon for a site to have multiple goals. If this is the case, it's important to identify which purpose is primary and which purposes are secondary. For instance, a site's main purpose might be to generate revenue, perhaps by selling sporting goods. Secondary goals might be to educate users about the rules associated with different sports and to provide entertainment with online sports games. The majority of your users will be drawn in by the primary goal. Secondary goals are often used as a means of engaging users (keeping them there) and retaining users (bringing them back). The combination of primary and secondary goals should affect the type of content and design you decide to incorporate.

Once you identify your site's primary and secondary goals, you can begin to establish the most appropriate design style, including when and where you should (and shouldn't) incorporate Flash. If the main purpose of your site is to educate users, then perhaps a Flash tutorial using animation and sound would be suitable. If the main purpose is to provide entertainment, then you might want to think about using Flash to create an interactive game. You should also be considering instances when, based on the goals you've identified, Flash, or excessive use of Flash, might not be the best solution. Be careful to avoid incorporating Flash simply for the sake of having Flash on your site. Flash, like every other element of your design, should improve the overall user experience associated with your site.

The Flash Gourmet: Creating a Delicious Dish

One way to think about Flash and its usefulness in your design is to think of your design as a recipe for a dish and to think of you, the designer, as the master chef. Your recipe for design will incorporate many different ingredients, such as color, multimedia, animation, images, and text. The key is to determine the appropriate use of each ingredient. To do so, you must understand the type of dish you're creating because this will play a part in determining the ingredients you choose to use. Think of this as the goal of the recipe.

After you decide on the type of dish you're going to create (the recipe goal), you also need to consider some information about the people who'll be consuming it. What type of people are they? How old are they? Where and when will they consume it? Suppose you decided to create a dessert for your eight-year-old nephew's birthday party, which will be taking place in your living room. Because it's a birthday party, a birthday cake would probably be most appropriate. And, because these kids are young, the dessert should probably be something that appeals to them visually by incorporating bright colors and designs. And, you'll want to forego the rum flavoring because, although it may be your favorite, young kids probably won't find it appealing. Because the party will be in your living room, you might want to go with a yellow cake (as opposed to chocolate) to minimize the potential for dark, chocolaty stains on your carpet.

Each of these decisions will make up the "experience" each child has with your dessert, from presentation to final consumption. Imagine what would happen if you decided a regular old birthday cake would be too mundane and decided, instead, on making an Italian tiramisu, complete with mascarpone cheese, coffee, and liqueur. Although tiramisu is a wonderful dessert, it's not really appropriate for a group of eight-year-olds.

This somewhat overly simple example is meant to illustrate a fundamental point. You need to consider a number of "ingredients" when planning and creating a site to ensure the final product is a success. Each decision is, in some way, focused around the needs and goals of both the product and the end user. If you fail to consider one or the other, you risk jeopardizing the success of your "dish." Worse yet, if you ignore both and create a dish based solely on your own personal goals and tastes, you'll likely end up with a product that suits only you. Are you prepared to eat all that dessert by yourself?

Provide Information

Sites that provide information are typically driven by large amounts of organized content. Some sites provide information on a particular topic (such as health, sports, hobbies, and so forth) while others, such as news sites, cover a much broader range of topics. For example, The Discovery Channel's web site (http://www.discovery.com) provides information specifically on topics relating to science, technology, and history. CNN's web site (http://www.cnn.com) provides users with the latest news on a variety of topics both nationally and globally. The goal of an information-based site is to provide a large amount of content in a way that enables users to locate the information they need quickly and easily. Typically, the interface required to do this is text based (because text is often the most efficient use of space on a web page) with a few images and advertisements scattered here and there. Whenever a large amount of text is involved, Flash might not be the best medium to present the information for the following reasons:

❭ Large amounts of text embedded in a Flash movie are usually somewhat difficult to read. Often Flash designers use small, anti-aliased text presented in textboxes that users must scroll through to read. Most users have trouble processing information presented in this format.

❭ Many users are interested in copying or saving information presented on these types of web sites. But, when the information is contained within a Flash movie, this is difficult, if not impossible, to do. Unless the developer has built some customized programming into Flash to enable these features, users are unable to bookmark, copy, paste, or print text from standard Flash movies.

❭ Information providers typically require a search engine to look through the vast amounts of content. To create search functionality in Flash, developers must separate the content from the Flash movies. Flash content can't be searched on its own as of version 5.0.

Flash does let developers build in special programming to solve some of these problems. Developers can opt for larger font sizes and enable a feature that lets the users enlarge the font size of the text within the Flash movie on their own. Flash can also be told not to anti-alias text and can be modified to make text selectable, so users can copy and paste it much like they could HTML text. Some drawbacks still exist, however, that can't be ignored. These capabilities are limited regarding how much HTML can be displayed—currently, very low-level HTML code is supported. And modifying the Flash content to enable features like these takes time. In many cases, taking the time to do this might be cost-prohibitive for a project that could alternately and less expensively be completed using HTML. Even in cases where modifications have been made, issues involving the layout of the text could still arise. For instance, most Flash movies are displayed in pop-up windows and text information is often laid out in small text boxes, requiring users to scroll even to read a short paragraph. A large amount of text displayed in this format is difficult for users to read and process.

Flash can be used in other ways to enhance the information being provided, however. The Discovery Channel's TLC web site (http://tlc.discovery.com) uses Flash to provide users with interactive tutorials on subjects that most users would otherwise never be able to experience. For example, users can currently access a Flash-based tutorial module titled "Cheater's Blackjack" (see Figure 3-1). It provides users with a behind-the-scenes look at how computers can be used to aid "cheaters" at swindling people out of their money in the game of Blackjack.

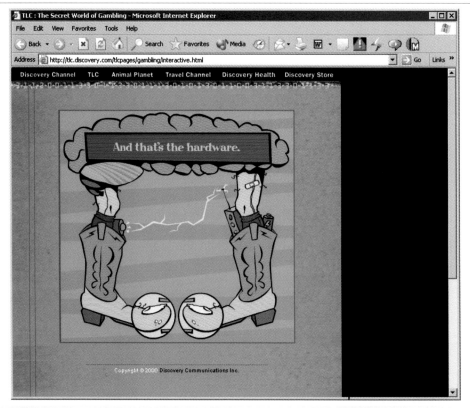

FIGURE 3-1

TLC's Flash-based tutorial, "Cheater's Blackjack"

Provide a Service

Sites that provide a service enable the user to complete a task through a web-based interface that, in many cases, would otherwise have been completed offline. For instance, PayPal (http://www.paypal.com) is an online payments service that lets the user complete the task of sending or receiving money to other individuals or businesses. Their service replaces the offline task of sending a check or money order to an individual or charging a credit card directly to a business. E-mail service providers, such as Hotmail (http://www.hotmail.com), enable users to send and receive electronic mail. Typically, sites that provide services are process driven as opposed to content driven. Users must complete a process (searching, sending, receiving, and so forth) in order to use the service or tool being offered.

In general, complex processes, such as an online purchase checkout process, aren't the best place to incorporate Flash. Flash animations can be distracting, and when users are trying to complete a process, distraction isn't a good thing. A distracted user might leave out an important piece of information or send information (such as an online payment or an e-mail) unintentionally resulting in inconvenience, confusion, or embarrassment. Because many service-related processes are, at some point, irreversible, users need to stay focused.

Notice we haven't said Flash should never be used in this type of a site. There's a time and a place for everything. You should use caution, though, if you decide to incorporate Flash elements, and remember, if Flash doesn't provide a positive addition to the user experience, you might need to question why you're using it at all.

Generate Revenue

Sites aimed at generating revenue are typically known as *e-commerce sites.* The main goal of an e-commerce site is to sell products to customers to generate revenue. Information about the products being promoted can also be provided on the site; however, the reason for providing such information is to facilitate the primary goal—selling products. Sites with an e-commerce focus almost always include a shopping cart function, which enables users to go through the process of paying for and setting up shipment of the items they're purchasing.

When thinking about where and how to incorporate Flash in this type of site, remember, users typically want to be in control of their shopping process. From browsing through an online catalog, to searching for a specific item, to completing the checkout process, users need to feel they're in control of their experience. Make sure by incorporating Flash, you don't take that control away from them. Few successful e-commerce sites are designed entirely in Flash. It's possible to design a usable e-commerce site entirely in Flash, but doing so can be tricky and, in many cases, can complicate the shopping and checkout processes with an overuse of animation. Additionally, although the majority of online users do have the Flash plug-in (97 percent according to Macromedia), not all users are comfortable with excessive Flash content, and using it as the platform on which to build an entire e-commerce site might exclude some would-be customers from purchasing products.

The majority of e-commerce sites with Flash use it as a tool to enhance their product offerings and to convey their brand image. When the user first enters the site on the home page, Flash can be used to promote brand image either by building the entire home page or as an addition to static content. On shoe retailer Journeys' web site (http://www.journeys.com), Flash is used on the home page to augment the surrounding static content by drawing attention to certain brands and products (Figure 3-2). It's used

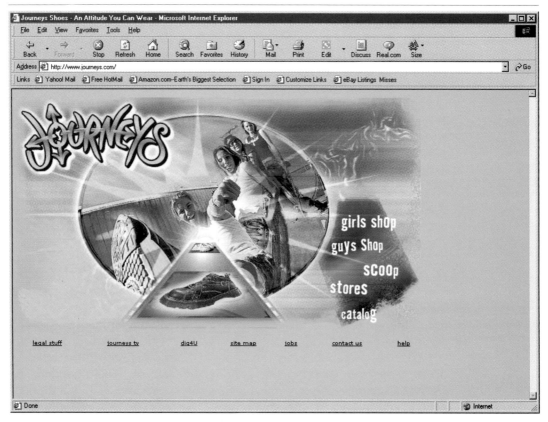

FIGURE 3-2

Journeys.com uses Flash on the home page to call users' attention to featured brands and products in an unobtrusive way and doesn't interfere with the users' ability to navigate through the site or the checkout process. Fossil Watches (http://www.fossil.com) also integrates Flash design into its site (see Figure 3-3). Instead of using Flash on the home page, however, Fossil Watches includes a small Flash movie presentation on the product category pages to call attention to a particular watch from that category. Again, the Flash movie is unobtrusive and doesn't distract the users away from the pursuit of their initial goal. Instead, it draws attention to a product the company is trying to highlight, similar to the way a point-of-purchase video display in a store draws attention to the product is represents.

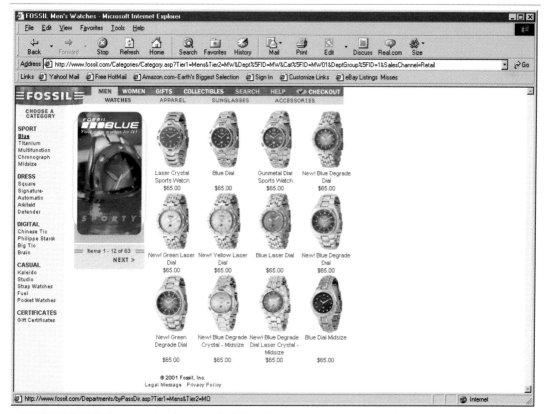

FIGURE 3-3

Fossil.com uses Flash to highlight featured products

Provide Education or Training

Education and training sites are sites whose primary purpose is to educate and/or train users on a particular subject. A site educates users by teaching them *about* something. Users are trained when they learn *how* to do something. Although both training and education sites might incorporate interactive elements to accomplish their goal, training typically requires more interactivity with users to be effective.

Flash can be an extremely beneficial tool when designing modules and interfaces to train or educate users. Flash can be used to create highly engaging educational movies and interactive presentations. To illustrate how important engaging your users is while you educate, think back to a class you had in school with a teacher who was dry and boring. Your mind most likely wandered during the lectures and you probably absorbed little of what was taught. Now try to remember a teacher who was just the opposite: one who captured your attention with interesting activities, movies, presentations, and teaching style. Because you were kept engaged in the class, you probably retained more of the information being taught.

Education works the same way online, except online it is even more important to engage your users because they can get up and leave the class with the click of a mouse button. When given the option between reading pages and pages of static HTML text and images or viewing a dynamic multimedia presentation, most users chose the latter for the obvious reason that it's more interesting. In addition, Flash-based tutorials usually provide a smoother information flow than HTML-based tutorials because information can stream in piece by piece, reducing the need for user intervention. A Flash-based interface does have the disadvantages of being more difficult to bookmark and print than a static interface, but these weaknesses can be overcome. Flash developers can break Flash movies into separate pages, each containing its own HTML page for each movie. This enables the end users to bookmark each section as they choose. As mentioned in Chapter 2, you can use the Macromedia Print SDK to enhance your site's printing capability, to make it better than a traditional HTML page.

New Media Giants put together a nice example of a Flash-based educational presentation titled "Kubrick2001: The Space Odyssey Explained" (http://www.kubrick2001.com), as shown in Figure 3-4. The presentation is offered in five languages and is made up of four five-minute long segments that examine and attempt to explain the themes of Stanley Kubrick's 1968 film, *2001: A Space Odyssey.* Users can view the presentation as a whole or choose a specific segment to view. The users are continuously presented with bits of information, from system requirements to load times to tips on how to make the presentation load quicker, to let them know what to expect in the functionality of the presentation. The information flows smoothly and

FIGURE 3-4

"Kubrick 2001: The Space Odyssey Explained" is a 20-minute Flash presentation that educates the user on possible explanations and themes of the Stanley Kubrick classic, *2001: A Space Odyssey.*

provides an engaging experience for users to learn about some possible themes associated with Stanley Kubrick's classic movie.

Behind the Scenes: Kubrick2001

Following is a behind-the-scenes look at some of the considerations that went into creating "Kubrick2001: The Space Odyssey Explained," as described by Graeme Thomas of New Media Giants.

Technical Aspects *We started with an elaborate storyboard, but had to progressively trim down our ambitions as we ran into the limits of Flash (mainly overly large file size and animations too complex for the average CPU). But once those limits were accepted, it became* *challenging to reduce every scene, sound, and animation to its bare essentials. The result might be laughed off a TV or cinema screen, but it works on the Web because users accept the current limitations of the medium.*

Site Statistics *Our web logs show that around 50 percent of visitors who come to the site see the "whole show," all 20 minutes of it. When you think of the number of possible reasons a visitor might "go elsewhere"—slow or expensive Internet connection, underpowered CPU, lack of time, lack of interest—the fact that we manage to hold half of these notoriously impatient Internet users for 20 minutes of "passive viewing" shows what Flash can do.*

Flash "Philosophy" *The best starting point for a Flash presentation is to have an idea, and then use Flash to express it. For our project, we completed our storyboard before we even started to learn Flash programming. Maybe there are too many Flash projects that begin the other way around—that is, Flash programming in search of an idea.*

Counterspace (http://counterspace.motivo.com/) is a Flash web site whose goal is to educate users on typography and its history. Users can learn how letters are constructed, how fonts are classified, the history of typography, and other facts. Virtually the entire site was created in Flash. And yet, contrary to the "too-busy, too-complex" perception many users have had of Flash sites in the past, this site is clean, simple, and easy to use. For example, in the "anatomy" section of the site (see Figure 3-5), when users roll their mouse over various character structure terms, the definition of the term appears and the related structural element on the letters below is highlighted to provide a visual explanation. User can navigate quickly from one term to another without having to wait for pages to refresh or new images to load. The same benefits are carried throughout the rest of the site, providing an engaging, efficient, easy-to-use educational experience for users.

Promote a Company or Product

The majority of business-related web sites fall into this category. Their main goal is to inform visitors about their company and the products or services they offer. These are marketing-based sites aimed at promoting a brand, product, or business. Whereas the main goal of the aforementioned service provider or e-commerce site is to generate revenue or enable users to complete a service-related process, the promoting site provides information about products and services, which are then purchased and/or consumed outside the web site experience.

Sites used to promote a company or product can use many different types of content to do so, including text-based content, 2-D and 3-D

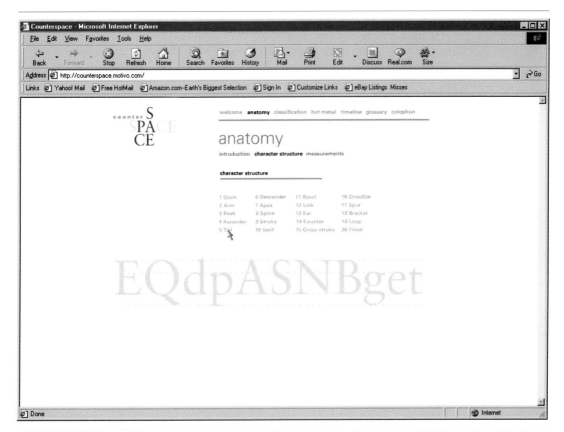

FIGURE 3-5

Counterspace uses Flash throughout its education-based site

images, presentations, and nearly any other element that might help represent the company and its products and services. The opportunities to incorporate Flash in this type of site are endless. To avoid misusing that opportunity, however, you must remember the type of company or product being promoted and the users to which you're promoting it.

Obviously, some sites will warrant the incorporation of more Flash than others. For instance, if you're designing a site to promote your personal portfolio of Flash design, as shown in Figure 3-6 (http://www.petergrafik.dk/ dubonet_retro_experience/), then by all means incorporate lots of Flash to show off your capabilities—just remember to make sure it's usable. In other cases, Flash can be used to add functionality and provide added detail about a company and its products. For instance, hair-styling product company Vidal Sassoon (http://www.vidalsassoon.com) uses Flash to enhance its Style Gallery (see Figure 3-7) by offering users the option to view a slide show in either animated format (Flash) or standard format (HTML). Download times for each version are provided to aid users in their decision. The animated version helps convey the company's creative, cutting-edge brand image; however, users who aren't interested or aren't able to view this version can view the same content as a static HTML presentation.

Remember, though, the user experience isn't made up entirely of functionality. Usability also factors into how visually engaging a site is, and Flash can be used to improve usability by improving a site's aesthetic appeal. Take, for example, Bennington College's web site (http://www .bennington.edu) shown in Figure 3-8. Flash is used throughout the site's

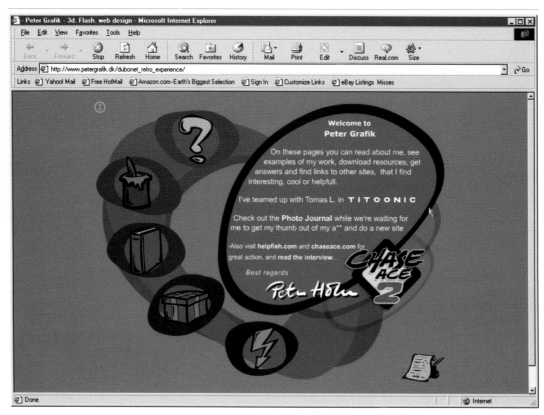

FIGURE 3-6

Flash-based online portfolio of designer Peter Holm

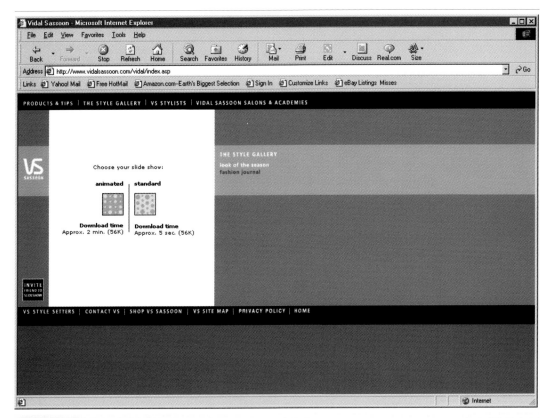

FIGURE 3-7

Vidal Sassoon's Style Gallery provides users with approximate download times for Flash and HTML slide show options

navigation to add visual appeal that you don't find on many university web sites. The navigation might have been just as functional had it used HTML or DHTML, but it probably wouldn't have been as engaging or conveyed the same brand image, which sets it apart from other competitor sites.

Provide Entertainment

As the title implies, the main goal of an entertainment site is to provide users with entertainment. Entertainment can be provided in a variety of different formats including movies, music, games, and interactive activities. Lilgames.com, a site that provides free online games, uses Flash to create everything from puzzles and sports games to 3-D action games. The company even has a Flash-based version of the popular "Simon" electronic

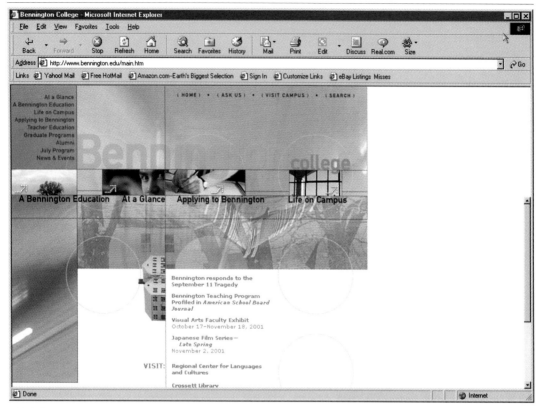

FIGURE 3-8

Bennington College uses Flash to enhance the navigation throughout its site

game called Simon Says (see Figure 3-9). Users see four large, colored panels. After the panels light up, each with an accompanying tone, the user's job is to replay the sequence by pressing the panels (using their mouse button) in the same order the computer did. The game continues until a sequence is repeated incorrectly, which triggers a buzzing sound and the game ends. The experience is so reminiscent of the original game, you might forget you're not playing with the real thing! This, like the other games on their site, is simple, easy to use, and loads of fun.

What's Her Face (http://www.whatsherface.com), an entertainment site targeting young girls, provides users with a number of Flash-based activities, including one called "Video Magic," which lets users choreograph their own music video by mixing and matching various dance moves and special effects (see Figure 3-10). The interface is unique, easy to learn, and provides an entertaining experience that wouldn't have been possible without the use of Flash.

Flash and entertainment go hand in hand. Entertainment is, by definition, something diverting or engaging. By nature, the tone or atmosphere of an entertainment site is more easygoing and artistic than other types of sites. Entertainment sites provide fertile ground for a designer's creative vision, and Flash provides the perfect medium to develop this vision into engaging content using animations, presentations, and games. Developing entertainment-based content is also an excellent opportunity to try out new looks, new functionality, and new ideas. Users will typically be more willing to

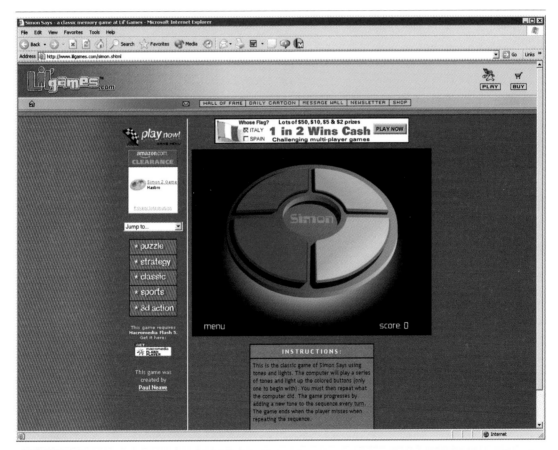

FIGURE 3-9

Lilgames.com's online version of the popular "Simon" handheld electronic game

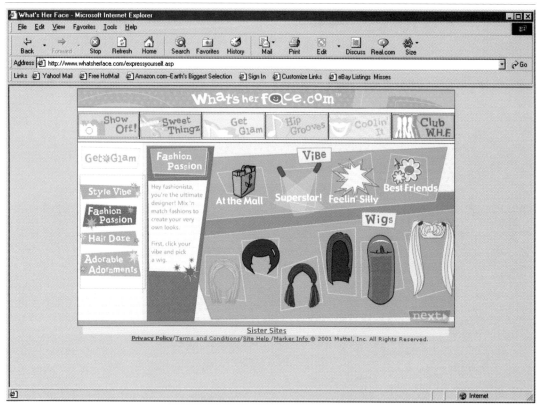

FIGURE 3-10

Whatsherface.com's interactive "Video Magic" Flash module lets users choreograph their own music video

take the time necessary to learn a new technology when it's entertainment-related, but they'll only do so if the interface is, indeed, "learnable." This is where understanding the type of users you're designing for becomes extremely important, as well as testing your site with representative users when it's finished to ensure they're able to use it. We discuss knowing your users next and we take a closer look at user testing in Chapter 6.

Provide a Portal

An Internet portal is a site whose main purpose is to act as a starting point for users to connect to other content on the Web. There are two types of portals: *general* portals, such as Yahoo, Excite, and AOL, and *niche* portals, such as Flash Kit, Boathow, and Office.com. Both general and niche portals offer similar services such as a directory of links to other web sites, a search feature, news, e-mail, and sometimes a community forum, but in a niche portal these services will be limited to the specific topic their niche serves.

Because of the volume of information contained on these sites, most portals have adopted the Yahoo-style of content organization with text-intensive, fast-loading pages that users find easy to use and to return to. Because portal sites are typically visited as a means to an end—they are a stepping-stone to another site—Flash content on portal sites is usually limited to banners and advertisements. In this case, Flash's animation capabilities are being used to catch the user's attention and get them to click on the ad.

Yahoo! It's Pizza!

In October 2001, Pizza Hut partnered with Internet portal Yahoo, using a Flash advertisment on Yahoo's home page to promote Pizza Hut's $8.99 Ultimate Lover's pizza. Upon entering the Yahoo site, users saw an animated Ultimate Lover's pizza pop out of the center of the page. The pizza then flipped over to the Marketplace section of the site, where it was integrated into a square banner-type advertisement. Users then saw pepperoni and other toppings sprinkle over the pizza. Clicking the ad's "Click for recipes" link triggered a Flash slide show of different versions of the Ultimate Lover's pizza. If the user continued by clicking through they were taken to Pizza Hut's "PH899.com" web site, where they could get more information on Pizza Hut's $8.99 pizza deal, download coupons, and play pizza-related games.

The entire process of the pizza appearing on the screen and moving to the right side column took only a few seconds. Plus, users weren't forced to take the time to close any unwanted pop-up windows—if they weren't interested they simply ignored the ad and within a second or two it was out of the way. By using Flash to create a compelling, interactive ad that integrated well with the site's content and functionality, Pizza Hut was able to market their product in a unique and innovative way.

Designing for the Main Business Goals: How and When to Use Flash

The success of a business depends on following clear guidelines to achieve a goal. Flash sites need to be part of a well-organized online strategy.

Information Provider

When a Flash developer is presented with creating a site that's content heavy, it's important to review your user goals. For the content-heavy site, the user goals are usually simple: search, retrieve, print, and obtain information. Anything like animation and buttons that make sound must be evaluated with these objectives in mind. Few information-driven sites require animation and sound, unless the animation is content itself, such as an animated diagram or a teaching aid. Many content-driven sites in the educational field benefit greatly from Flash animation to help illustrate problems and complex topics better. Flash is helpful to content providers if it's used to display complex information that would be rather hard to display in traditional HTML format. For instance, a site that offered economic data could use Flash to produce real-time 3-D bar graphs that are updated based on live stock data. This would enable end users to view information in real time in a graphical format. Good Flash animation can help illustrate or support the user's actions. For instance, if users click a Print button, the Flash movie can offer an animated icon appearing to print, with a short sound. This would provide feedback to users that their action has taken effect.

Service Provider

One of the areas where Flash is starting to be applied is the Application Service Provider (ASP) market. ASP developers have traditionally used advanced HTML, frames, and JavaScript to create front ends for their web services. These companies provide services such as company intranets, Web Mail, Content Management Systems, Billing Managers, and Time Entry systems, which all function through a browser. Now Flash is being used as a front end to some of these systems. By using Flash instead of traditional HTML and graphics, ASP developers can create complex customized interfaces that feel more like traditional desktop software than web pages. By creating web applications in Flash, they can make the programs easy to use and more impressive looking to help increase sales. Also, by using Flash, ASP developers can deploy web applications across multiple platforms with less debugging and workarounds for different versions of browsers and operating systems (OSs). Flash delivers to ASP developers what Java promised: platform independence.

E-Commerce (Revenue Generator)

E-commerce sites can benefit from Flash as a means to enhance product demonstrations and visualization. One of the largest drawbacks most consumers feel when using the Web to shop is the lack of interaction with the desired product. Many users enjoy handling or lifting a product before they purchase it. Web developers can now use Flash to let consumers have more interaction with their product. With Flash, you can get closer to satisfying three of the senses, instead of only the visual sense. An excellent example of how Flash is used to showcase a product is on the Palm site (http://www.palm.com), where users can explore and have a simulated experience of what the Palm OS feels like. Users can open the cover of a Palm and navigate through its easy-to-use and well-designed interface, all from the comfort of their own homes. Computer-related products have benefited greatly from Flash media because their complex qualities can be reproduced using Flash's ActionScript and graphics capabilities.

Flash is also a good medium to use in an e-commerce site that sells a service. Often, there isn't product to ship or deliver, so it's a challenge to sell a service online that takes place after the sale. Flash can be used to show steps in a process or to provide an interactive diagram illustrating how the service is beneficial to the end user. Before the use of Flash, such services could only use primitive animated .gifs and static graphics to display a complex service.

Education/Training Provider

Flash has enormous possibilities for the educational field. A new generation of students has come to expect a higher degree of sophistication from the material presented in school. The age of overhead projectors and acetate will soon come to an end. Teachers in high schools and post-secondary schools are beginning to understand that captivating and high-impact technologies, such as Flash, can increase student learning. Many schools use Flash not only in educational web sites, but as supplements to other technology, such as PowerPoint. PowerPoint remains one of the key tools used by teachers because it's easy to use and requires no scripting to put together a simple slide show. Flash is often used as embedded objects within PowerPoint to display a complex animation impossible to create within PowerPoint itself. In university settings, academic departments often have resource departments that can produce specialized animation required to explain a complex problem. The professor can then take these animations and insert them into PowerPoint for use in the classroom. Although Flash is a robust tool for the creation of interactivity and animation, it's often too difficult for teachers to learn how to use. But, once mastered by the educator, Flash can prove a valuable tool to create educational animation that would traditionally cost thousands of dollars to purchase. Instead of having to purchase expensive videotapes, cash-strapped schools can now produce their own set of learning materials.

Corporate training has benefited the most from Flash technology. Companies can now engage their employees with interactive modules, instead of making them sit through hours of boring videos. Using Flash over an intranet, companies can review employee's scores, as well as collect data necessary to improve production and the actual training process. In a large food chain located near Detroit, Michigan, employees in central facilities located near their stores are trained how to bag groceries. These facilities all draw their training modules from one central location via an intranet. Flash is used to animate the proper way to bag groceries: employees learn to bag eggs and other breakables separately. At the end of the training, the employees see their scores and their numbers can be reviewed by the employee and the supervisor to see where improvements can be made. Employees enjoy taking the training because it's interactive and has a game quality to it.

Company or Product Promotion

Flash has seen the greatest use in the area of product and company promotion. In some ways, Flash got a bad name from information architects because of the gratuitous use of Flash to make company logos spin or branding tag lines slide on a page. Many developers who first start working in Flash resort to the "Flaming Logo" style of web design. The Flash development scene is, however, maturing, and companies are now using Flash to help engage and retain their target audience. Brands such as Adidas are using Flash to create more than pretty animations. At the site, myadidas.com (http://www.myadidas.com), the company presents the users with a CD-ROM–like experience that allows them to travel through a world retrofitted to match the brand of shoe they're interested in. The target audience for this site is obviously younger, thus the sounds, graphics, and interactivity are all cutting edge. Adidas leverages this "space" to help promote the brand identity of the shoes, and helps users become interested in purchasing based on branding and the "cool factor."

Entertainment Provider

The entertainment industry probably uses Flash more than any other industry. This is because Flash is a natural extension of their animation and storytelling skills. Movie sites are now used as interactive trailers to help build momentum in advertising and marketing campaigns. Flash can be used to build portals dedicated to animated cartoons. Many sites feature interactive weekly features exclusively online. Flash has transformed the Web from a purely information medium into a source of entertainment. The goal of most entertainment providers is to engage the user and to provide some type of content that brings users back or encourages them to spend money in the movie theatre. Well-designed campaigns created by entertainment providers offer users some direct relationship between the Flash site and the secondary goal. For instance, several entertainment sites

Q & A Interview with Dr. Mike Atkinson, Professor of Psychology, University of Western Ontario

How have you used Flash animation to illustrate complex information?

I've used Flash to illustrate how light is transformed into vision in the human eye and how neurons influence each other.

Have you replaced any traditional classroom media such as PowerPoint or videos with Flash animation?

We have used Flash to supplement PowerPoint. Flash can be used to create animations and is customizable in ways that would be difficult or impossible to achieve with PowerPoint.

Give us some examples of how Flash animation enabled you to accomplish something that would otherwise have been impossible across the Web?

Flash enables me to demonstrate complex concepts and to create engaging web materials that result in more interactive learning and, consequently, greater comprehension of the material. Flash also enables me to synchronize audio, video, and text on the Web.

Why do you use Flash instead of digital video?

Flash requires less bandwidth than digital video to deliver full-screen presentations. Concepts that would be difficult to illustrate using video are easy to illustrate in Flash. There are also things that would be difficult to present with Flash that are easy to do using video. It means using the most appropriate tool for the required outcome. Flash gives me one more tool to get the job done.

feature cartoons. At the end of every cartoon, viewers are told the time and date of the next full episode on TV. These multimedia campaigns are successful because they reinforce the message. Some entertainment sites, such as Star Wars.com (http://www.starwars.com), serve as a platform to fuel interest and excitement for upcoming movies. The Star Wars' site builds excitement and interest by offering interactive Flash content, such as a tour of Anakin Skywalker's home. Users are able to view stage sets used to create *Star Wars: Episode One.* This creates excitement and helps build the Star Wars brand.

Who Are Your Users?

Once you establish the purpose of your site, you need to determine who the users of your site will be. A positive user experience can mean different things to different users, so to provide a positive experience for your users, you need to know something about them and what they'll interpret as positive. You need to develop a solid understanding of who they are, their abilities, limitations, needs, goals, and expectations. Each of these aspects will influence when, where, and how you incorporate Flash into the design of your site.

User Characteristics

First, it's important to determine the goal of your site, so you can get an accurate idea of who might want or need to visit it. In some cases, this will be relatively easy and obvious; in other cases, it might be difficult to pin down an exact set of users. For instance, if you're designing a site like the previously mentioned whatsherface.com (Figure 3-10), it's obvious your key user group will be young girls. If you're designing an e-commerce site like amazon.com, which sells everything from books to patio furniture, however, you'll have a much broader, and therefore more difficult to define, set of users. In either case, it's helpful to start by breaking down your users into user groups. A *user group* is a set of users defined by a common trait or characteristic. You might have only a few users' groups, or you might have several. Once you determine the various user groups for your site, it's also helpful to identify which group or groups make up your primary users and which are secondary.

As you strive to gain a better understanding of your user groups, try to document every detail about them that could have some bearing on the way they interact with your site. This is called *profiling* your users. We'll provide a list of typical characteristics to evaluate when developing your user profiles. Depending on the goal of your site, you might decide to add or subtract from this list. Typically, you need to complete one user profile per user group. For example, if you're developing a web site to promote your personal design services' portfolio, you might determine you have the following three user groups:

❯ Companies interested in hiring you

❯ Individuals interested in hiring you

❯ Other designers interested in viewing your work

In this example, you would want to complete three user profiles—one for each group profiling an actual representative user from that group. A set of thorough, on-target user profiles can guide you and keep you on track through the design and development of the site.

The following summarizes elements of a user profile:

❯ User objective (the reason the user is coming to the site)

❯ User expectations (what the user is expecting from the site—graphics, functionality, features, content, and so forth)

❯ Age

❯ Sex

❯ Nationality/Primary language

❯ Geographic location

❯ Occupation

❯ Familiarity with and frequency of using the Internet

❯ Familiarity with programs plug-ins, such as Flash

❯ Browser

❯ Type of computer and equipment (hardware and software) being used

❯ Internet connection speed

❯ Level of education

Browser Considerations

One of the greatest strengths of Flash is its cross-platform reliability. Creating this cross-platform reliability isn't always as simple as publishing the source Flash to a SWF. Developers who have spent years working out the page-rendering differences between Netscape and Internet Explorer will know that each browser type and version has its own unique way of rendering pages. Although Flash reduces this problem immensely, it does not completely eliminate it. For instance, the screen real estate displayed by Internet Explorer and Netscape is slightly different by almost five pixels. When developers are creating Flash content that needs to be restricted to

Personal Viewpoint
Check Across Platforms

Working as a Flash developer for large agencies has taught me many lessons. But the most important lesson I learned is to check my Flash movies across platforms as they are being developed. Before I started work I was asked what software I needed. After that was squared away, I would say I needed a Windows test machine to check my work. This request was often met with hostility by the IT department because they didn't understand why a "creative" needed a PC. I would arrive to work and find the latest and greatest Mac sitting on my desk with no Windows machine to be seen. After a few weeks, I would be up and running, and in the thick of developing Flash media. My supervisors would review my work on Macintosh computers and approve the work for client review. We would bring an Apple laptop to a client meeting and show the client the work, the client would approve the project, and it would go live. At this point, the Flash media hadn't received any serious testing

on the Windows platform (with the exception of being reviewed on personal computers at night). Flash movies we created often looked fine on Windows, but we had horizontal scroll bars and content that disappeared off to the right of the screen.

After several months of such problems, the IT department installed several machines in a public area for people to test on. These machines had different versions of browsers and Microsoft Windows installed on them, which helped the situation greatly. Many of the Flash developers used the machines regularly to check their design ideas. Our horizontal scroll bars started to disappear and our Flash movies began to look great on Windows. This resolved many of our problems, but it didn't eliminate them all. The test Windows machines saw increasing use, and often would be down because of all the conflicting software being installed for testing purposes. Our team requested having a Windows machine placed on each Flash

developer's desk to speed testing and insure timely review of content. Once again, because of budget restraints, politics, and the usual large organization grind, our requests met resistance.

As a workaround solution, the IT department installed Windows emulator software on our Macs and told us that would be a good way to test the Flash media. Windows emulator software is excellent, but it is not the ideal way to test Flash media for delivery on Windows machines. We began to discover that Flash animation and screen redraw behaved like a 486 computer in this emulation environment. Finally, after many months of serious meetings and many internal e-mails, a budget was established for every Flash programmer to have a Macintosh and a Windows computer as standard issue. The result was faster development time and better quality Flash content. The money the company spent on several Windows computers was saved tenfold on the reduction of project overruns and redesigns.

–Kevin Airgid

the dimensions of pixels, these types of differences need to be taken into consideration to avoid unsightly horizontal scroll bars in the browser window.

Flash developers often make the mistake of designing a layout based on how a Flash movie looks in only one browser. In many design studios and advertising agencies, Flash developers are working exclusively on Macintosh computers. Although the Macintosh computer is a superior platform for creating graphics and multimedia, the Apple OS displays some Flash content differently than the average target audience using the Windows platform. Many of these developers often lack easy access to Windows machines to test their Flash movies. The result is Flash movies that create horizontal scrolling for users with 800×600 screen resolutions. Even when a movie is only five pixels larger than the viewable area, the browser draws a horizontal scroll bar to display the last five pixels hidden off to the right of the screen. As a result of this mishap, important navigation items, such as a Home button, are often hidden offscreen for the user. You can rectify some of these problems by setting your margin widths and heights to 0 (zero) in the body tag of your HTML file, which will cause the Flash movie to fit flush against the browser padding.

Screen Real Estate Keeps Changing

One of the most frustrating things about developing Flash for the Web is that even the same browser can have different screen real-estate sizes. What we mean by *screen real estate* is the actual pixel dimensions the browser has to display your web content. The current standard for developing sites is 800×600 screen resolution. Most national-level sites now use this standard as the minimum resolution for the general public. (You will find some sites still using 640×480, but these are the exception, not the rule.) 800×600 is generally agreed upon as a safe benchmark to design your Flash site around, but what about browser real estate?

When a home user purchases a PC, turns the computer on, and connects to the Internet, usually the browser and OS are set to a default configuration. This configuration often has extra tool bars turned on, which most users don't know how to turn off. Some installations of Internet Explorer have a radio toolbar turned on. This toolbar can consume around 10 pixels of the vertical screen real estate. Also, by default, the Windows Start menu is always set to on. This consumes more precious screen real estate. Many Flash developers are advanced OS users: they customize their Windows configurations such as setting the Start menu to auto hide and turning off seldom-used toolbars in the browser. This affects the development of Flash media because the developer has more screen real estate than the average user, which leads to problems with design and usability.

A good idea when designing your Flash content is to test your design on as many different types of browser configurations as possible. Even turning off and on seldom-used toolbars in the same browser can give you an idea of how much screen you'll have left in a worst-case scenario. You can solve many of these issues by creatively using hidden frames and setting your Flash movie to scale by percentage, rather than setting it to a fixed pixel height and width. By setting your Flash content to scale and stretching to the browser window, you reduce the concern about Flash content being hidden, but drawbacks exist in setting your content to scale. By having your content scale, animation plays more slowly because there's a large screen to refresh. If the screen resolution is set extremely large, your design will appear too big on large monitors. If you intend to develop your content with many raster (or bitmap type) images, you probably won't want to set your movie to scale by percentage because the raster images will appear both distorted and low quality as they scale past their original size. Whether setting your movie to scale by percentage or setting it to a fixed width and height depends on the media you plan to display and your target audience. Once again, your target audience should always be your priority.

Equipment Considerations: Hardware and Software

Imagine you're designing a Flash site for users with a slow Internet connection. Many of these users connect using a free (banner ad–driven) Internet provider. This free service installs a large banner ad toolbar on the screen, consuming both screen real estate and download bandwidth. For this example, the average user is running a computer with the following software configuration:

⟩ Windows 98

⟩ Internet Explorer 4.0 (default toolbars on)

⟩ Permanent banner ad at top of screen

⟩ Flash 4.0

The average low-end hardware configuration is

⟩ 15-inch monitor

⟩ 4MB video card

❯ 32MB RAM

❯ Pentium II 200 MHz

❯ 800×600 resolution

❯ Thousands of colors (high color)

❯ 56K modem

The client wants to use Flash to enhance their product and ensure the content is interesting and fun to explore. It's important for the content to run the same on the base machine, as well as on faster computers. A good idea on how to begin designing such a site is to get access to a computer that has the same configuration before you start designing. If you can't get access to such a machine, try setting your development computer to similar settings. Even if you can't change your browser for an older version, you can still set back your monitor resolution and color depth to match your target audience. Even this simple step can help you understand how this environment behaves. If you're fortunate enough to access a good example of a test machine, use this opportunity to surf to other Flash sites and observe how this machine behaves under different examples of Flash animation and interactivity. What types of Flash animation work best? Observe which sites run faster and which run slower. Write down what sites perform the best and those that perform the worst. Take a screen capture of the target screen with the banner ad running and all the toolbars set to the default position.

You can use this screen capture as a base for your design concepts. Import the screen capture into your favorite design program, and then use this screen capture as a template for your design. It will also ensure you contain your main design elements and navigation to a highly visible area. Remove the content from the screen capture and place it on the topmost layer. You can now design in a virtual window of your target audience. Flash designers often make the mistake of designing a site without relating it to the final screen. The many layers of default gray in the toolbar affects how the overall design looks on the screen. To ignore busy banner ads and default toolbars could negatively affect both the design and the usability. As a Flash developer, you must become sensitive to the frame the browser creates around your content. If you know the target audience is going to have a busy banner ad at the top of the screen, adjust your design accordingly.

The target audience should be the focal point for your thought process when developing a Flash site, especially when hardware and software are on the lower end of the charts. Now we've discussed screen real estate, but what about animation and interactivity? Our target audience for this example has 32MB of RAM and a 4MB video card. We know basically what is loaded into memory: Windows 98, Internet Explorer 4.0, probably other autoinstall items such as Norton AntiVirus Autoprotect, and other little taskbar applications.

Task Bar Memory Junkies

Have you ever used your friend's slow computer—you know, the friend who doesn't know much about their computer and yet has installed every piece of software from every free CD-ROM that came with their computer? When you turn on the computer, it takes ten minutes to boot up because it has ten little hogs that load into the bottom right of the Windows Start menu. Fun little programs that change the desktop pattern every five minutes, tell the time in England, and pop up a quote of the day. You wait patiently for all this to load up, and then you connect to the Internet to show them your cool new Flash animation that now runs like a snail because they have bloated their mid-end computer system with memory suckers. Well, rest assured, your friend isn't the only person with type of problem ... so be careful with how much animation you use in your Flash movies. It might be running in snail mode on your target user's computers.

You can figure a lot of the 32MB of RAM is probably consumed loading these basic things into memory and there probably isn't a whole lot left over for your fancy new Flash animation. When you add more complex animation and interactivity to a movie, you create more demand on the CPU, video memory, and RAM of the client computer. A low-to-mid-end system will have far less memory available than expected, so always underestimate what your host machine can handle. Our example has a limited budget for video memory and for RAM, as well. So, our Flash movie must be limited in its use of animation.

You can still create a movie with elegant animation, but you must test it often on your base machine and keep your frame rate low to achieve this. A good idea is to storyboard out animation sequences on paper to test your ideas and concepts before you attempt execution. Think about how you might attempt to develop these animations and how you can use low-frame rates and smaller animation areas to create the same effect. Because the target computer probably won't be able to sustain a high-frame rate, you should limit the animation to a smaller area of the screen. By creating a smaller screen area for the animation, you're reducing the screen area the computer needs to redraw to produce the animation, which helps the computer draw the animation faster. Also, in this case, a good idea is not to let the movie scale by percentage because this increases CPU and video RAM use as the computer has a larger area to redraw. Using a fixed-size movie, setting the width and height by pixels, would be best. A trick to creating fuller-looking animation is to fill the screen with static graphics that match the animation and only animate a small portion of the screen. This will give the visual illusion that the whole screen is part of the animation. Our lower-end computer will only need to redraw a small portion of the screen, but to the viewer the animation will look like part of a larger scene.

Finally, for this low-bandwidth example, we need to discuss interactivity. Flash ActionScript is, for the most part, forgiving when it comes to CPU use. Flash ActionScript is much better than other technologies, such as DHTML and Java Applets. But when you apply complex ActionScripts to graphic elements, you're once again demanding much more from client CPU and video cards. You can get many free ActionScripts from Flash developer sites, such as Flash Kit (http://www.flashkit.com), that enable you to apply complex actions to graphics dynamically. Some of these impressive ActionScripts can make images wobble or appear to have gravity effects. Although these impressive little ActionScripts might work fine on a developer's computer, they might not cut it for our target audience. Be sure to test these scripts early and often on your base target computer before you apply them to a whole site that's almost finished. Showing an interesting ActionScript effect to a client, only to find out later it can't be used on your target machine because it demands too much hardware use, is painful. Even things as simple as dragging a symbol with a bitmap embedded in it across the screen can be too much for some computer systems.

Internet Connection Speed (Broadband vs. 56K)

A user accessing your site through a broadband connection will have a different experience from a user accessing your site through a 56K dial-up connection, especially when the site includes graphics and animations that require a lot of bandwidth to download. Users aren't patient people. They come to your web site with needs and goals to accomplish, and have expectations as to how long this process should take. Generally, a user will wait a maximum of about ten seconds for a page or element (such as a Flash animation) to download. Of course in some cases it's much shorter, but when a user feels that waiting for the download will enhance their experience and facilitate the accomplishment of their goal, they are much more likely to wait longer. This likelihood can be increased even more if users are provided with some indication of how long the wait will be.

Many Flash sites use a simple blinking Loading message while the movie downloads; however, this doesn't tell the user how long the loading sequence will take. A user left wondering if the movie will take a few more seconds or a few more minutes will often abandon the process before they ever find out. A better option is to provide the user with a graphical depiction of how much of the animation has loaded and how much remains. Even better—give the user something to do while they wait and they'll be less likely to keep track of the seconds ticking by. Basilisk Interactive, a Flash-focused interactive design company, does an excellent job of this (see Figure 3-11). A user can move their mouse to change the animation while the site loads. This site isn't anything sophisticated, but it does a good job of distracting users, so they aren't as aware of the time required for the site to load. When the element is one the user has the option of downloading, it's also helpful to state the size and/or approximate download time. Vidal Sassoon's Style Gallery does a nice job of this (shown earlier in Figure 3-7). Users have the option of choosing either an animated (Flash) or static (HTML) version of a slide show. Approximate download times are shown for each.

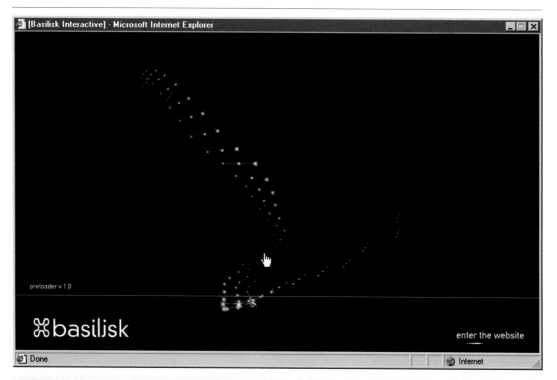

FIGURE 3-11

Basilisk Interactive engages users with interactivity while its Flash site loads

Streaming vs. Loading Flash Content   Streaming Flash content is one of the key features that enables developers to create bandwidth-friendly sites. By *streaming* in parts of a Flash movie, the Flash developer can give the end user the capability to view and interact with a Flash movie before it's completely downloaded. Streaming is more effective than making the user wait until the movie is 100 percent loaded. Flash developers can use streaming to load in important items, such as main navigation, before an image or a short animation sequence is loaded. This enables the users to start using the site right away if they want to continue on to a different part of the site without having to wait for the rest of the movie to load. Another good technique is to load essential elements, such as navigation, titles, and small photos, first on the main movie. Then, if you have a large audio track you want to play, stream this clip in after the main elements are loaded. The users won't notice because the music will slowly stream in the background as they explore the movie.

Once again, it's important to test early, test often, and test under different conditions. Even though streaming music might work properly on your DSL or cable connection, it might in fact slow the loading of secondary movies on a 56K connection. Test how your streaming works on slower target machines. If your sound track is extremely large, it might reduce the speed of your site, and then you'll have to decide if the music truly adds value to the site. If you must include an audio track in your site, a good idea would be to use ActionScript to test for the speed of the connection. You can then load your audio track if the users have enough bandwidth to accommodate a larger audio track. If the users are using a 56K dial-up connection, you can instruct the Flash movie to download a smaller, lower-quality track to achieve the same goal. By doing a little scripting up front, you're creating smart streaming content and enhancing your users' experience.

Abilities and Limitations

Different user groups will have different capabilities and limitations. Understanding what types of limitations your users might have is important, so you don't exclude key user groups with design elements that make the site unusable to them. Also important is to understand your users' capabilities to avoid detracting from the users' experience with an overly simplified design.

Some capabilities and limitations depend on characteristics like age, familiarity with the Internet, type of equipment, and education level. An Internet-savvy user might be able to understand how to navigate your site with a little help, while someone less experienced might need more explicit directions to navigate. A user connecting to your site through a broadband connection and using the latest in computer technology will have capabilities a user connecting through a 56K modem using the computer he bought four years ago won't have. Other capabilities and limitations might be based on physical conditions. For instance, color blindness, hearing impairment, physical handicaps, and other conditions can limit what a user is able to view, hear, and accomplish on your site. So that you don't exclude users with physical handicaps, make sure a user wouldn't have to rely on a design element, such as color or sound, to navigate your site. These elements can still be included, but you should be aware that some users will be viewing and using your site without them. (For more information on design considerations for physical conditions, see Chapter 6.)

When deciding when and how to incorporate Flash into your design, it's extremely important to remember these capabilities and limitations, particularly the limitations. Rarely do designers have a problem with their designs being too simple. Problems most often arise when designs are too advanced for the intended audience. The majority of designers are using the latest and greatest equipment with huge monitors and high-speed Internet connections. Although a Flash-intensive site design might work well with the designer's knowledge and environment, actual users who don't have such advantages could find the same site unusable.

Needs, Goals, and Expectations

Users will come to your site to fulfill a need or desire, or to accomplish a goal. The purpose of your site, along with the characteristics of your users, can help you determine what these needs, goals, and expectations are. For example, if the purpose of your site is to entertain, the majority of your users will probably visit to fulfill a desire for entertainment. If your site is e-commerce focused, the majority of your users will come to purchase something they need or want. Before even coming to your site, many users will develop an expectation about what they'll find when they arrive, based on the purpose of the site, as well as their own needs and goals. A user visiting a news information site, such as CNN.com, expects to find mainly text-dominated pages of well-organized new items, while a user coming to a site offering entertainment probably expects to interact with engaging graphics and animations. This isn't to say you shouldn't ever include Flash animation on a site where a user might not expect to find it. If you choose to do so, though, be sure the users' initial needs, goals, and key expectations are still being met and that, in incorporating Flash, you've added to their experience by making it better than they expected, not worse. In short, the best uses of Flash are the ones where users don't even realize they're using Flash. When Flash is used to better an online experience, the technology behind the interface will seem almost transparent to the users. And, when they're done, they might not even recall they were using Flash, but they will recall the great experience they had.

In many cases, users come to a web site with a preconceived notion of how the site will (or should) meet their needs and goals. Remember, how users interpret their experience on a site will be made up of more than how easy it was for them to accomplish a task. It will also be influenced by their expectations. The contrast between users' expected experience and their actual experience will have an effect on their attention span, patience, and overall satisfaction with their experience on your site. Users tend to have longer attention spans, more patience, and feel most satisfied when the actual experience most closely matches the expected experience. When reality matches expectations, it provides users with the sense of security about the environment they're interacting with. When it doesn't, users tend to feel what they're experiencing is out of their control and they'll try to do whatever they can to regain a sense of control—even if this means shutting down and leaving the site.

When you design a site, it's crucial to design with your users' best interests in mind. You need to remind yourself constantly of their characteristics, capabilities, limitations, needs, goals, and expectations. We've said this before and we'll probably say it again—Flash is a tool, a tool that should be used to make something better. In other words, the experience a user has should be better with Flash than without it. If this isn't the case, then you need to rethink why you're using Flash in the first place. If you ever question whether your design will provide a positive user experience, use the information you've collected about your users as your guide and your measuring stick. The old saying "measure twice, cut once" could be revised in this case to read "measure twice, design once." If you take the time to learn about and understand who you're designing for and to measure your design constantly against that guideline, you'll save yourself time (usually closely related to money) in the end by eliminating usability problems, which can result in lost customers (users), reduced sales, and time-consuming site redesigns.

Summary

Defining site goals and user goals sets the foundation for creating a usable design. A solid understanding of the purpose of your site is intended to help you develop an initial idea of the types of design elements that might be appropriate. It can also help you accurately define the types of users being targeted. Understanding who your users are—their needs, goals, capabilities, limitations, and expectations—can lead you toward better understanding the most-appropriate design elements and type of design and can lead to a positive overall experience for the user. With a solid foundation in place, you can begin creating and building a usable design. In the next chapter, you have a more in-depth look at navigation and the ways in which Flash should (and shouldn't) be used to enhance a user's navigation through a site.

Flash Usability Fast Facts

> Determining the purpose or goal of the site you're designing provides an initial basis for understanding the most appropriate ways to incorporate Flash into your design.

> A site can have multiple purposes, including a main purpose and one or several secondary purposes.

> When determining who your key user groups are, understanding their characteristics, capabilities, limitations, needs, goals, and expectations is important.

> Connection speeds, hardware and software, knowledge, and physical handicaps all pose limitations to what some users are able to view, hear, and accomplish on the Internet.

> Test early and test often on your target computer configuration.

> Streaming Flash content is one of the key features that enables developers to create bandwidth-friendly sites.

> Users are more likely to wait for a Flash site or animation to download when provided with a status indication showing how long the loading sequence will take to complete.

> Flash is helpful to content providers if it's used to display complex information that would be hard to display in traditional HTML format.

chapter **4**

Flash Navigation: The Good, the Bad, and the Ugly

Web site navigation systems are made up of various elements. In this chapter, we explain how each of these elements relates to the graphic design and overall usability of the site. We identify areas in which Flash can be incorporated to enhance the usability of navigation systems and instances in which Flash can hinder a user's capability to navigate effectively. By looking at examples of usable and unusable Flash navigation design, we hope to provide you with an understanding of how to use Flash appropriately and how to avoid frustrating your users with overly complex designs. The goal of this chapter is to help Flash developers understand that form and function can coexist to create aesthetically pleasing, well-organized, usable navigation systems.

Importance of Navigation

Good navigation is important, regardless of the technology used, because it is the main control of your site. Think of your navigation as if it were the steering wheel of a car. The steering wheel in most cars is circular and easy to wrap your hands around. Regardless of whether the car has power steering, the wheels move when you make the necessary turns to control the car on a road. The navigation for your site needs to be viewed in this light. Flash designers, in their creative spirit, often create complex, yet beautiful, navigation systems, but because of their complexity they aren't usable. To use the analogy of the car steering wheel, this would be like creating a steering wheel from red Jell-O. Although the steering wheel might be visually appealing, it would be hard to use. These Flash designers fail to understand that navigation is a vital tool users need to explore the content of the site. Without placing usability on a par with design, the Flash navigation system will crumble and become a red Jell-O steering wheel.

Many leaders in the information architecture field have polarized design from usability. Some would lead us to believe that a totally usable web site is a site devoid of any design or graphics, and one that lets you navigate the text with tabs. A web site without design is like life without art. The world would be a gray and dreary place without artists' input into even the most mundane things we use each day. Our toasters—even our cell phones— have had a designer review them, and enhance their color and shape to make them more appealing to own and use. The Flash developer needs to take this approach to navigation design. How can the Flash designer enhance the navigation so it's comfortable to use for the target audience, yet turn shape and color into something the user can enjoy. The two ideas seem opposed to each other. Form versus function should not be the issue. Flash designers need to see past the rhetoric and view usability as a creative problem. Just as Flash designers solve color and graphic problems, they need to approach usability as a creative problem rather than a roadblock to good design.

As you begin to design your interface for your Flash site, you need to review your site's objectives. Who is your target audience and what is the most effective way for them to navigate the content? A good idea is to have a list of these goals in front of you as you design. If you're designing on paper first, lay out the goals of the site in front of you. If you're using a computer, try using sticky notes attached to your monitor to remind you of the goals of your site. Another good idea: take your target audience and the goals of your site, and from them distill a list of navigation and technical rules your Flash site must follow.

Types of Navigation

Before we dive into all the nuts and bolts of creating a usable Flash navigation system, it's important to understand the different types of navigation systems that might be incorporated in a site. At one time or another, most designers have heard terms like primary navigation, subnavigation, and global navigation. Designers need to understand the characteristics and differences between each type of navigation system to design and incorporate them successfully. In the following overview, we use Bennington College's web site (http://www.bennington.edu) to help illustrate and clarify the nature and usefulness of these various navigation systems (see Figure 4-1).

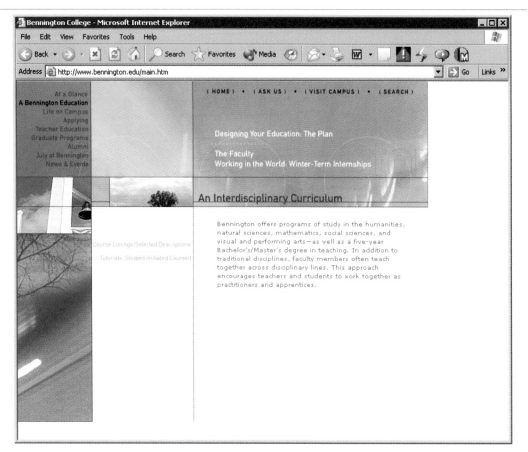

FIGURE 4-1

Bennington College's web site was designed entirely in Flash

Primary Navigation

A site's primary navigation is typically constructed using an *information hierarchy,* which forms the basis for organizing content on a site by using a treelike structure. An information hierarchy has multiple main categories that should lead to the categories of information users are most likely to seek on your site. These main categories make up the site's primary navigation. Each element in the primary navigation should be a link to a main category of information within the site. Under each main category, you might have several subcategories (they make up the primary category's subnavigation system) and so on. All content contained on the site is then organized in a hierarchy under the primary navigation categories. The primary navigation system should be the most prominently located navigation system and be available to users at any point in the site. Regardless of how far users have drilled down into your site, they should be able to access primary navigation links without having to return to the home page. In our example shown in Figure 4-1, the group of category links on the far left-hand side of the page is the site's primary navigation.

Some designers like to use Flash to conceal the primary navigation on various pages within the site. When a user leaves the home page, the primary navigation might be concealed under a button with the label Menu or Navigation. Users must click the button to reveal the primary navigation. Some usability experts argue adamantly against this practice, saying hidden navigation should never, under any circumstances, be used. In general, given the choice between a hidden and a consistently visible (always-on) navigation system, always-on is the better (and safer) option. However, this is not to say there is anything inherently unusable about concealing the navigation. As long as users have a clear and simple way to access the navigation whenever they choose, a concealed navigation system can be executed in a manner that doesn't detract from the site's ease of use.

If you decide to use a concealed navigation system, you'll need to look closely at the labeling and location of such a feature to ensure that users are able to find it easily and understand what to do once they've found it. For instance, using an abbreviation to label the navigation tool, such as Nav (the abbreviation for navigation), isn't a good idea because many users won't be able to make the association instantly between the abbreviation and actual meaning. Above all, remember to consider the audience you're designing for. Regardless of how noticeable and understandable you design a concealed navigation feature, some users still will have a difficult time using it. If you feel this might be the case, play it safe and stick with the more common always-on primary navigation.

A good idea, generally, is to limit the number of primary navigation categories to no more than nine. The point of limiting the number of categories to nine is to avoid overwhelming users with too much information at one time. Obviously, instances will occur when this isn't possible, and then you need to use your best judgment (along with the other concepts we've discussed) to provide users with a comprehensible primary navigation system.

Subnavigation

A site's *subnavigation* system is made up of subcategories to the primary navigation system. Primary navigation elements operate throughout the site and are always visible to the user, but subnavigation elements typically operate and are visible only within the pages of the primary category that contains these elements. Subnavigation might be made up of either category or content links, depending on the size and depth of the site. In a large site with multiple levels of information, subnavigation systems are typically made up of links to subcategories of the primary navigation. In our example, the subnavigation is made up by the list of subcategory links in the upper middle/right section of the page.

Designing Your Education: The Plan
An Interdisciplinary Curriculum
The Faculty
Working in the World: Winter-Term Internships

Some sites have more than one level of subnavigation, known as *local navigation.* In our example site, if users were to click An Interdisciplinary Curriculum, they would see an additional level of navigation, as shown in the next illustration, specific to and viewable only from that local section of the site. This navigation is made up of links to content specific to that subnavigation system.

Course Listings/Selected Descriptions

Tutorials: Student-Initiated Coursed

Sub- and local navigation systems are useful because they help organize a site's content in a logical format and provide users with an understanding of that organization. This is especially true when a site's navigation uses the Web's hypertextual capabilities, allowing users to link from one set of local navigation to another (*lateral navigation*) without drilling down through primary categories of information (*vertical navigation*). Too much lateral navigation can obscure the organization hierarchy and leave users feeling lost and confused. This tends be a common problem with sites that incorporate a Flash-based navigation system. The animated, unpredictable nature of many Flash-based designs, combined with a failure to provide users with a well-defined navigation structure, can easily leave users feeling as though they've stepped into an amusement park fun house. Building on a clear, well-defined local and subnavigation system is one way of helping users navigate through your site without getting lost.

Global Navigation

Like a site's primary navigation system, the global navigation system is available to the user from any location in the site. The difference between global and primary navigation is that *global navigation* typically doesn't have subnavigation. Global navigation is usually made up of direct links to standalone pages and sections that users might want to jump to at any point during their visit to a site. Common global navigation categories include Home, Contact Us, Search, Site Map, Help, Shopping Cart, and Checkout. These are processes users might want to get to quickly and directly (such as Search or Checkout) and/or pieces of information they might want quick access to (such as Contact Us or Help). The following illustration shows the global navigation system used on the Bennington College web site. The categories the college chose to include in its global navigation system include Home, Ask Us, Visit Campus, and Search. Global navigation systems should be located distinctly, but less prominently than the primary navigation.

[HOME]   •   [ASK US]   •   [VISIT CAMPUS]   •   [SEARCH]

Common Usability Standards for Navigation

A site's navigation is arguably the most important feature in determining whether the site is usable. Navigation breaks down the content on a site into sections, enabling users to find the specific piece of content they seek. Navigation is the user's road map to everything contained in your site. Whether users are shopping for and purchasing products, playing interactive games, or searching for a news article, the navigation system determines whether this process is frustrating and painful, or straightforward and painless. No matter how cool, creative, and wonderful a site's content is, if the navigation fails, the site will probably also fail because users won't ever find the majority of that content.

Sites incorporating Flash into the navigation tend to have particular usability problems because, by its nature, Flash encourages designers to "break" common usability rules for navigation. Flash enables the designer to have room to play with moving pieces on the screen much more easily than ever before. But Flash does little to remind designers of the "rules" they should follow as they play. As a result, many designers have been carried away "playing" with the navigation, which results in difficult-to-use sites.

You might wonder if you're going to be bombarded with a long list of usability do's and don'ts—the kind that threaten to sap every bit of creativity from your designs. Put your fears to rest. The intent of this section is to discuss some common usability guidelines as they relate to navigation and to help you better understand how these guidelines can effectively (and creatively) be incorporated into a Flash-based navigation scheme.

Location

In discussing navigation, location seems one of the biggest areas of debate between designers and usability experts. Many usability experts feel the *top and left standard* (placing navigation at the top and down the left side of a page) is the only way to go. Users are familiar with top/left navigation and, therefore, it's generally easy for them to use. On the opposite end of the spectrum are the designers who love to be creative with virtually every aspect of a site's navigation scheme, including where and how it's located on the page. Incorporating Flash makes straying from a standard navigation scheme even easier and more tempting. Sticking with one single location for every site's navigation would take away an element of creativity most designers aren't willing to give up. And so, the debate goes on.

So, which side is right? Should navigation be located in the same spot on every web site in existence? Or, should the standards be ignored in favor of coolness and creativity? The answer is both sides are right.

The reason so many usability experts argue for the standard top and left navigation scheme is it has become just that—a standard. Users have become familiar with finding the navigation at the top or left of the page and, therefore, many sites continue to follow this format. In addition, because most people, at least in North America, are accustomed to reading from left to right and top to bottom, formatting a site's navigation in this way makes sense and is very usable. Users, especially inexperienced users, feel more confident and in control of the interaction when they can locate a familiar navigation structure on an otherwise unfamiliar site. This provides them with a place to start and a sense of direction. This standard navigation format also works well for sites that contain vast amounts of content, such as the information provider sites discussed in Chapter 3. Placing the navigation at the top and/or left of the page creates a neat, clean, and organized page, and in some cases this is exactly what you need.

That said, let's look at this issue from the designer's point of view. To start, assuming designers would consistently follow a standard that often goes against the nature of their job (being creative) is unrealistic (come on—how many graphic designers do you know who live by the rules?). Additionally, strictly abiding by this standard is sometimes unnecessary and, in a few cases, doing so might prevent a user from having a positive experience on the site. Do you remember how this standard came about? The original purpose was to help create a navigation that was easy to recognize, easy to understand, and, therefore, easy to use. Plenty of sites are on the Internet today that use nonstandard navigation schemes that are still recognizable and easy to understand. And plenty of sites use the top/left standard navigation scheme and are still difficult to navigate because of other usability problems.

In our experience, the physical placement of navigation on a page isn't the main factor in determining whether users can navigate successfully. Other factors seem to play a much more important part in determining the usability of a navigation scheme. Following are some criteria that can help to ensure a usable navigation scheme.

Guidelines for Usable Flash Navigation

To ensure usability, navigation should be recognizable, learnable, consistent, and traceable.

Recognizable   Recognition has to do with whether users can identify navigation elements as navigation. In other words, when users come to your site, can they easily determine the links that will lead them to the content they're looking for? Many Flash navigation schemes suffer from being overly creative and, thus, unrecognizable as navigation to users. Examples include the following:

> **)** **Hidden navigation**   Navigation labels that remain concealed or unclear until users move their mouse over them.

> **Abstract navigation**   Navigation that fails to follow any type of logical, distinguishable format in structure, labeling, or both.

> **Moving navigation**   Navigation that continually moves on the screen, often forcing users to chase links before they can select them.

Such navigation schemes force users to move haphazardly around the screen, hoping for a clue that might point them toward an element of navigation. In most cases, users don't enjoy this tedious process of seek and find.

The good news is navigation doesn't have to be boring and dull to be usable. You can incorporate usability standards into a creative navigation design to make sure users can recognize and understand it. Use design elements to separate the navigation from the content on your pages, so users aren't confused by what's content and what's navigation. Use Flash to introduce the navigation on each page where it might not be obvious at first. Call attention to a concealed navigation scheme with pointers or indicators that purposefully state Menu or Navigation. Remember, regardless of how creative and cutting-edge your navigation is, users must be able to find your navigation and understand how to use it for it to be effective. Otherwise, they'll never make it past your home page.

Learnable   Navigation should be easy to learn. Users should be able to learn and remember how to use a site's navigation with little cognitive effort. Part of making navigation learnable is incorporating good labels (we'll discuss these in an upcoming section), so users can easily predict and remember where a click will take them. Navigation that fails to meet the first criterion of being recognizable typically fails to meet this criterion as well. Let's look at an example of an unlearnable navigation scheme.

Figure 4-2 shows a grid, which consists of a square on a black background, sectioned off with thin white lines into nine identical smaller squares. Although the designer attempted to make this navigation scheme recognizable by providing a label, users are given no indication of what they can navigate to. Users must click on a square and wait for that section to fill the page before they know where they've navigated. Once there, users have no means of getting back to where they came from unless they remember the last square they clicked on and select it again. Remembering which square leads to which section of the site is next to impossible. Imagine how you would feel if you were in a house whose main room had nine doors on one wall. To go into any other room in the house, you must use one of those nine doors. Only after opening a door, proceeding through, and closing it behind you could you find out where the door led. Once in the room, you turn around to see the same nine doors on the wall behind you. To go back to the room you came from, or to go to any other

FIGURE 4-2

This navigation system hinders usability by requiring users to remember what section of the site each square will take them to as they navigate

room, you must remember which door led you into the room and which doors lead to other rooms. How frustrating! You'd feel so lost and confused, you'd decide to leave the house completely (assuming you could even get out at all, that is). This is exactly how users feel when they're presented with this type of unlearnable navigation—lost and confused.

The bottom line is this—most users don't spend nearly as much time on the Internet as those who design the sites they visit. Therefore, although you might have no trouble learning a particular navigation scheme (especially one you designed), users might have a much more difficult time grasping it. Sometimes users simply need a bit of tutoring. Flash provides an excellent means of providing tutoring features. Using Flash animation, a designer can animate a cursor to demonstrate to the user exactly how to perform certain tasks, including navigation, on the site. You generally should only need to provide this type of tutoring once during a user's visit (normally on the home page). If you find your users require further or repeated explanation, your navigation is probably too complex and needs to be simplified for them to learn how to use it effectively. Remember—if users can't learn it, they won't use it. And, if they don't use it, they can't be considered your users. What's the point of having a site without any users?

Consistent   Consistency plays a part in determining how learnable and recognizable a navigation scheme is to users. If the navigation scheme lacks consistency and is constantly changing in its look and/or location from page to page, users will have a difficult time recognizing the navigation when they move to a new page. They might even wonder if they're still on the same site. Inconsistency also requires users to relearn the navigation whenever it changes. Some designers make navigation inconsistent to "fit" it within their design. Others feel it adds an element of creativity to their design. Regardless of the reason, inconsistent navigation isn't a good idea.

We'll use an example to illustrate this point. Imagine you went into a video store to rent your favorite movie. You'd expect to find videos and DVDs displayed in an organized, logical, consistent manner. But, what if you went to the Comedy section and found one subsection for comedy videos and one for comedy DVDs, both organized alphabetically. In the

Action/Adventure section, however, videos and DVDs were mixed together and organized according to release date. Moving on to the Drama section, you discover the video selections organized by the leading actor's last name and the DVDs are nowhere to be found. You'd probably find navigating through this store's content extremely confusing, and after a few minutes of searching for your movie, you'd probably leave and head for another video store.

The same principles described in the example apply to the Internet. Inconsistency causes frustration and confusion—two things most users hate and won't tolerate. Most users would rather leave a site than waste their time wandering through inconsistent navigation.

Because of the animated, movement-oriented nature of most Flash designs, navigation inconsistencies can quickly become a problem. Designers often incorporate Flash as a means of animating elements on a page, including navigation. Consistency doesn't mean navigation must remain completely static and identical from page to page. Consistency means maintaining the logic, organization, and overall look throughout, so users can easily recognize and learn where the navigation is located and how to use it to move from page to page. Avoid disorienting your users by providing them with a consistent means of moving throughout your site.

Traceable   Traceable is a word you don't often hear associated with a site's navigation. A *traceable* navigation system is one that provides users with the capability to retrace their steps. Virtually every user has experienced wandering through a site, click after click, only to wonder, "Where am I?" Users can get lost easily, especially on sites that contain large amounts of information or on sites that use a nonstandard navigation scheme. It's important to aid navigation and provide feedback to users to help them avoid that lost feeling. Features that enable traceability aid navigation by providing users with a sense of where they are within a site. A number of graphical and textual conventions can be used to accomplish this.

Graphical conventions include the use of elements such as color, highlighting, font size and style, underlining, and indicator icons (such as pointers, arrows, and bullets) to provide at-a-glance information to users on their current location within a site. In Figure 4-3, it's easy to see where you are on this T-shirt retailer's site. The site uses graphical elements, such as color and shading, to indicate your current location, which happens to be SnugWear T-Shirts> The Baseball T> Cotton> Green. You're looking at a green shirt in the subcategory Cotton of the local navigation category The Baseball T, which all fall under the primary navigation category of T-shirts. Users can easily navigate back to any section within the hierarchy by selecting the highlighted link on the page shown.

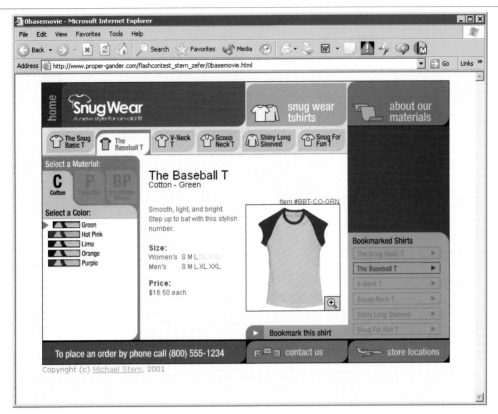

FIGURE 4-3

This Flash-based T-shirt retailer's site uses graphical elements to indicate the users' location in the site as they navigate

By using Flash, designers also have the capability to use animation and movement to convey "you are here" information to users. For instance, when a user clicks a primary category link, the selected link might move to the top or the beginning of the primary navigation structure to show the users they're currently in that section. A word of caution if you decide to use Flash animation in your navigation structure: remember, in using Flash, you must maintain consistency and avoid hindering a user's ability to "learn" the navigation system. Navigation systems constantly moving around on the page or incorporating abstract animation sequences ultimately do exactly the opposite of what you might be trying to accomplish, leaving your users confused and unsure of how to navigate through your site's structure.

The most popular textual convention for providing traceability is the use of breadcrumbs. No, we're not referring to the crumbs on your keyboard that have accumulated from one too many working lunches. *Breadcrumbs* are a textual representation of where the user is in a site that enable a user to go back to any previous category simply by clicking it. Breadcrumbs should be located near the top of the page and usually look something like this: Home> About Us> History. Two types of breadcrumbs can be used. The dynamic Hansel and Gretel type of breadcrumbs track a user's actual steps of progression through the site. If a user takes six steps to get to History (that is, Home> News> Press Releases> Recent> 50th Anniversary> History), the breadcrumbs will show every category visited.

The more common and, we believe, more useful type is a *hierarchical breadcrumb* display, which represents the structure of content within the site. Using the previous example, regardless of how a user managed to get to History, the breadcrumbs would show the location of the History section within the site's hierarchy (that is, Home> About Us> History). This type of breadcrumb display is helpful because users can then navigate backward to find other related sections of information. For instance, a user could now go back to the About Us section and find other related information contained in this category. A hierarchical breadcrumb display also shows users the most logical and direct path to a section within the site, which supports the process of learning the navigation system. The following illustration shows an excellent example of an actual Flash design that incorporates breadcrumbs into the navigation.

<u>Home</u> > <u>Company</u> > <u>Careers</u> > Benefits

Don't Break My Back Button

Perhaps one of the most important features of a traceable navigation system (and most often overlooked by Flash designers) is the browser's Back button. Many users consider the Back button their safety net—it is perhaps the most useful and most used feature for recovering from errors when navigating through a site. Disable the Back button and you've just taken away your users' last resort for jumping out of where they don't want to be. As you're probably well aware, sites designed entirely in Flash typically don't allow access to the browser's Back button because, unlike HTML-based sites, Flash sites aren't made up of individual web pages, but are one continuous movie. As an alternative, some designers place their own Back button within the pages of their Flash site, providing users with an alternative when the browser's Back button has been disabled. This option is certainly better than no Back button at all, but users are most familiar with using the Back option from their browser's toolbar.

Enabling the Back button is possible, even in a site designed completely in Flash. It requires the use of frames and passing variables from the browser to the Flash movie. As Flash loads each movie into a new layer in the base movie, the browser loads a hidden frame. By loading hidden frames, the browser can build a history of where the user has been. When the user presses the Back button on the browser, the hidden frame tells the Flash movie to go to the proper frame of the parent movie. Teaching this topic is beyond the scope of this book, but Robert Penner offers source Flash, HTML, and JavaScript files about this topic at his site located at http://www.robertpenner.com.

Labeling

We mentioned earlier that the navigation system was the road map for your site. The labels given to each element of navigation, also known as the labeling system, are the road signs. As users navigate through your site, interacting with and searching for information, they need signs along the way to point them in the right direction, suggest paths, and mark destinations. How you label these signs will play a major part in determining a user's ability to make wise navigation choices—choices that will take them where they want to go. Problems arise when designers decide to get a bit too creative with their labeling systems. Labels affect how learnable a site's navigation is. When labels are clear, concise, and easily understood, users have an easier time learning the navigation. When labels are ambiguous and unclear, users have a difficult time understanding which navigational elements will take them to the information they want. Users shouldn't have to spend their time trying to determine what each label is supposed to mean. Following are some criteria to help ensure a usable labeling system.

Guidelines for a Usable Labeling System

To ensure usability, labels should be descriptive and self-explanatory.

Descriptive   Labels should provide an accurate description of the content they represent. Just like a street sign along the road, labels need to tell the user where they'll end up if they choose the path indicated by a particular label. Choose labels that provide users with the information they need to stay on the right path in their quest for information. Avoid choosing vague labels or those or that could easily be misinterpreted. Users shouldn't have to guess about the purpose of a link or where it will take them.

Self-Explanatory   The meaning or implication of a label should be absolutely evident to the user. Users shouldn't have to *pogo stick* (jump back and forth between pages) through your site, making their best-guess navigation choices to find what they're looking for because the meaning of the labels you chose isn't evident or logical to them. And, remember—

While visiting a web site recently, I clicked on a link labeled About Us. I was hoping to find some information about the company, such as what it did, its history, and the location of its regional offices. I found none of these things. Instead, under About Us, I found information on product warranties, shipping and delivery policies, and a privacy statement. I clicked a few other labels, hoping to come across the information I wanted. I never found it. Maybe it wasn't there to begin with. Maybe it was in some other equally mislabeled section. The world may never know …

–Stephanie Reindel

different people interpret language in different ways. A variety of factors, including age, sex, nationality, educational background, and familiarity with the Internet, may affect how a user interprets a label.

Try to use labels your users will be familiar with and that won't be easily misinterpreted or misunderstood by the different user groups in your target audience. If you're having doubts about the labeling system you've chosen, test it. Put the labels in front of a few representative users (who aren't already familiar with your site). Without providing any additional information, ask them to tell you what they would expect to find or do after clicking on each label. The results of your test should make it obvious as to whether your labeling system is self-explanatory.

Text vs. Iconic Labeling Systems

The question often arises as to which type of labeling system is better to use—text-based or icon-based (iconic). Typically, designers will tout iconic labeling systems while usability specialists advocate text-based systems. In reality, there's no right answer. Both approaches have their own unique advantages when used correctly, and studies have found a combination (icons with text) is often the most effective. Of the three choices, though, iconic labeling systems are prone to the greatest number of usability problems, so we'll focus on that here.

I was on a site recently that used "Shout" as a navigation label to take users to a contact/feedback form. The designer was obviously trying to be creative and different, and came up with this unique label, rather than sticking with something typical like Feedback or Contact Us. It was different all right—but not all that evident, especially when I was scanning the navigation quickly looking for a way to contact the company. Sometimes, different is good; sometimes, it's plain confusing. I "shouted" a few of my opinions once I found the form.

–Stephanie Reindel

Although icons might look cool and fit nicely into your design, they're easily plagued by a variety of usability problems. For an icon to work effectively as a label, users must be able to interpret its meaning. Different images will represent different things to different users. For example, what do you think this image represents?

Perhaps it's a link to company contact information. Or perhaps it's a link to reports or printed material. Or maybe this icon represents something else entirely. The point is, depending on their background, users will interpret images differently.

Some icons have developed as standards to represent certain labels, such as a house to represent Home or a picture of a shopping cart to represent an online shopper's selection of items, but other labels are much more difficult to convey visually. Icons for these labels are typically difficult to recognize and decipher. For instance, a variety of examples of different icons have been used to represent a site map, including a picture of a map, a road sign, and a tiny hierarchical structure. Most users aren't able to associate a site map with a particular image or icon. Users typically overlook unclear icons as they scan the page for familiar elements.

One way to avoid interpretation problems with an iconic labeling system is to augment each icon with a text label. As mentioned earlier, research has shown the combination of an iconic label with a text label is better than either by itself. The text label might constantly be visible or it might only appear when users moves their mouse over the icon. In either case, this can help provide a clear interpretation of the icon and what it represents. In Figure 4-4, you can see an example of this. When a user moves their mouse over any of the icons, a text label is displayed to clarify the icon's meaning further.

If you choose to restrict text labels to appear only when the user rolls over the icon, you might also find it helpful to provide an animated demonstration of this for users upon entering your site. By briefly showing the frames in your movie that contain each text label—either one by one or all at once—you can help eliminate possible confusion regarding the location or the interpretation of the navigation system.

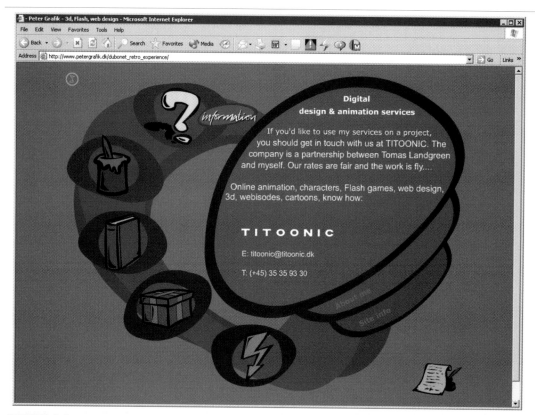

FIGURE 4-4

As users move their mouse over each iconic label, a textual label is revealed, eliminating confusion and misinterpretation of the images

Shopping with a Wheelbarrow

A few years ago, a web site that sold gardening equipment learned the hard way about the problems that can arise from using unfamiliar iconic labels. (Worth noting—this company is no longer in business.) In the top corner of its site was an icon of a wheelbarrow. The wheelbarrow was supposed to represent a user's shopping cart.

After analyzing log reports and finding that many users were bailing out of the site after adding a few items to their shopping carts, the company decided to do some research. What it found was many users were looking for the more-familiar icon of an actual shopping cart and

failed to interpret the wheelbarrow icon as such. When they couldn't locate the link to their shopping cart, they gave up and left the site. As a result, the company lost thousands of dollars in potential sales.

The wheelbarrow image might have been clever, but it wasn't familiar to users and didn't do the job it was intended for. Shortly after learning of the problem, the wheelbarrow disappeared and a good old-fashioned shopping cart took its place.

Some Problems Commonly Found in Navigation Systems: Focusing on Flash Navigation

For some reason, many designers seem to think that because they're using Flash instead of HTML, every aspect of the site (especially the navigation) must be unique and totally different from all other web sites. Much of this stems from the ability to create fancy, sometimes complex navigation systems that aren't possible using HTML. Caught up in creative freedom offered by Flash, designers can easily forget one very important aspect of navigation—beyond being "cool," it must be functional. The following are a few of the more common problems that occur when using Flash to create navigation.

Overused Animation

Flash navigation is often hard to use because many developers attach animation to simple navigation items. Countless Flash navigation systems force users to endure sounds and highly complex animation when the user simply moves their cursor over a button. Most of the time, these interesting animation sequences add little value to either usability or the design of the site. In the end, these animation sequences annoy the user more than anything else. The "gee-whiz" factor is lost after the second mouseover. Flash developers need to keep their eyes on the prize: the goals of the site and the target audience. If the animation doesn't add value, it needn't be there.

Poor Hit Zones

Complex animation isn't the only problem that plagues Flash navigation: small hit zones for buttons is another. Too often, developers create buttons in Flash that require hunting and exploration to find the hit zone. This problem occurs when the Flash developer doesn't create a large-enough hit zone inside a button. Developers who use all uppercase pixel fonts in the navigation compound this problem. Typically, these fonts are around 10 points and smaller. Although pixel fonts might be the rage on the typography scene, they make poor navigation text. The average user is now viewing sites at 800×600 screen resolution. Type smaller than 10 points is extremely hard to read even for users with 20/20 vision. Consider picking fonts above 10 points and try keeping the individual navigation items separated visually. Many Flash designers create minimalist navigation systems that have words floating in space. A good idea is to break up these navigation words with graphic treatments, such as lines or some other method, to identify that each item is separate. Each word might represent a different navigation item to the design team, but the end user might visualize the navigation as one big sentence if the design isn't treated in a method to indicate each item is a hot spot.

Task-Based Navigation Systems

Avoid task-based navigation systems—systems that require a user to complete a process or task (beyond a simple click) to navigate. Some Flash developers feel showing their Action Script abilities is important by writing complex, task-driven interfaces. An example of such a task-driven interface is a portfolio site that requires the user to pick up an icon of a video tape and drop it into a picture of a VCR to watch a piece of digital video. This might seem like a fun way to navigate a site, but it creates many problems. New users won't understand the "real-world" principles you're applying to your Flash site because they've been trained to click a button and receive information. You're now challenging everything they've learned to navigate information.

If you must use navigation that requires the user to drag an object over another object to navigate, include clear instructions on how to do this. Provide a mock user animation to show users what to do. And, if possible, include a secondary navigation in the form of text in case users become frustrated and don't want to relearn a new navigation system. Many HTML-driven web sites include text links at the bottom of every page, so users who have images turned off can still navigate the site if the navigation

Often when I'm creating a Flash site, I jot down a group of rules I must follow when designing the navigation. This keeps me grounded, so I don't create a navigation system my target audience won't understand how to use.

Here's an example of some site design rules:

Basic target audience: Men ages 35–45, middle class, 56K modem

Site Rules:
) Flash 4 plug-in only (ActionScript limited to 4.0 only capabilities)
) 4.0 browser
) Fixed moie 700×1500 pixels
) Forward button and Back button must work

) Breadcrumbs (because the site has many layers)
) Average computer speed
) 56K connection (small SWF sizes)
) No sounds
) Content colors will change, so navigation must be kept neutral
) No frames

–Kevin Airgid

is embedded in an image map. Flash developers should consider this feature for complex Flash movies. Providing alternative forms of navigation is essential if the navigation system is extremely different.

When and How to Bend the Guidelines of Navigation

Flash designers can often get away with bending navigation rules if they employ well-thought-out strategies for teaching users how to use their "new" navigation system. If you choose to do this, you should be sure your target audience is open to more creative navigation systems, and has the experience and patience required to learn such a system. If, for instance, you're developing a site for older teenagers, say 17–19 year olds, you might be able to enjoy more creative freedom with your interface. This target audience is typically more technically savvy and enjoys experimenting with new navigation systems. As we've mentioned throughout this book, you must begin by knowing and understanding your target audience and focusing your design on their needs and goals. If you decide your design cannot live without a hidden navigation system, you must make certain your target audience can use it without difficulty.

The Amnesty International 40th Anniversary Flash movie has a nontraditional navigation system (see Figure 4-5). It requires users to scroll horizontally to view the history of Amnesty International. Because the target audience for the site is broad, it was important for the site to be easy to use. When the movie first loads, it plays a animated help system over and over, until the user clicks the horizontal scroll bar to view more information. The

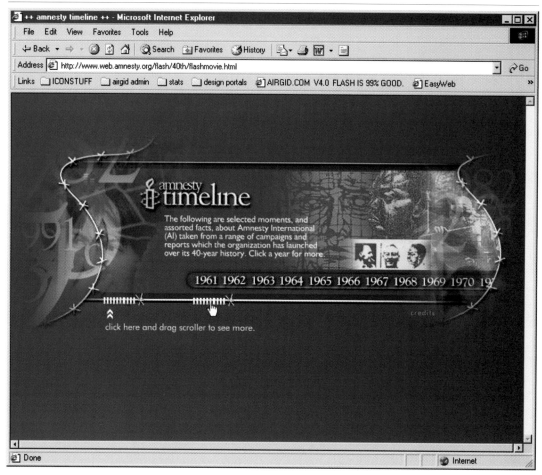

FIGURE 4-5

Amnesty International Help System (copyright 2001, Amnesty International)

help system uses both text to explain how to use it and a simulated cursor, clicking the scroll bar and moving it. By combining both text and visual feedback, the nontraditional navigation system has a better chance of being understood and used. Flash developers need to understand that if they spend hours developing a creative navigation system, they need to spend the same amount of time ensuring it's easy to use and learn. Making users learn new navigation systems every time they enter a site is not the best practice. We must caution that navigation design rules should be broken with extreme care.

Q & A Interview with James Baker of WDDG

James Baker is the founder and creative director of WDDG, an internationally known and highly awarded interactive firm in New York City. James has been an active participant in the Flash community for over four years. He has spoken at international conventions on the subject of Flash development and has contributed to numerous books on the subject, including the Flash 5 Bible. James's work has been recognized with awards from Communication Arts, HOW magazine, Macromedia, and FlashForward. He's currently developing a new gaming platform that merges the best that online gaming has to offer with offline elements.

What was the rationale for designing your site (http://wddg.com) completely in Flash?

Each medium that you can use to construct a web site has its own strengths and limitations. As the industry evolves and matures, we're getting a better grasp of these strengths and limitations. With the latest incarnations of the WDDG home site and with some client sites that we have developed like Maverick.com, we have attempted to capture the strengths of HTML and DHTML within a Flash interface. We wanted to combine the usability of an HTML site with the control and cross-platform functionality of a Flash interface.

How have you addressed the following usability issues?

❭ Users who don't have the Flash plug-in

❭ Users who are using older, slower equipment

With penetration for the Macromedia Flash 4 plug-in at close to 98 percent, we can safely assume the great majority of our audience has the capabilities to view our site. We do, however, provide a detection script that prompts users who do not have Flash 4 installed to do so. We typically have shied away from Flash 5 because of its lower rate of adoption. If you compare what we've done with WDDG.com and Maverick.com to a "typical Flash site," you will see what we're doing is much closer in look and feel to a "typical HTML site." We avoid transitions and unnecessary animation, and many of the other pitfalls that have made Flash sites such a despised concept. So, with less of the typically processor-heavy animations and transitions, we're creating sites that don't tax older machines.

Was any initial user research done before creating and launching your site? If so, what type?

We always do research before we make it to the design process. Research is an absolute must if you're hoping to achieve your goals. Although we generally don't have the resources to organize focus groups on what users are looking for, we do go out and research as thoroughly as possible what other people and companies are doing and have done, and try to take the best from each of those ideas and combine them into our approach. Sometimes nobody is having success or is doing a good job, so we start with a truly blank piece of paper.

Why did you create Flash sites such as Maverick.com and WDDG.com that enable users to scroll the Flash content in the browser window?

This is one of those instances where we paused for a second and tried to approach a problem from a different angle. Maverick wanted a stylish site that was heavy on content. HTML wasn't going to cut it in the style department. DHTML is a nightmare. And a Flash site was only going to obscure relevant data behind numerous clicks, transitions, and inertial sliders. We reasoned that more users know how to use a scroll bar than know how to use any Flash site interface, so we made the pages flow and scroll, and left all the content on the screen. I think that in the future, you're going to see many more sites like this.

Out of all the Flash sites you designed, which site do you feel has the most usable navigation system and why?

I'd like to preface this by saying we still have a great deal to learn in terms of interface design and navigation systems. I think most of our recent sites (Maverick and WDDG) have had strong navigation and usability, but this is more because we've been getting back to the basics. We pruned back all the bells and whistles, and designed sites any user could immediately navigate. Immediate feedback and transitions, clear navigation, and an interface that doesn't need a help section can only help to make your site clearer and easier to navigate.

What types of navigation systems do you like? And what types do you hate? And why?

I like navigation systems that fit. There are millions of different ways to navigate information or to navigate a site. The trick is to apply some thought to what you're trying to accomplish with your navigation, what the information is structured like, who your audience is, and what their experience and preconceptions are like. I like interfaces that are clean and clear, have good information hierarchy and design, and can immediately be recognized as navigation systems. These ideas are more common sense than rules that someone has laid out. The first goal of your navigation should be navigation, not aesthetic beauty.

When you're designing a Flash navigation system, what's your first step? Do you sketch it on paper or start by diving into design software?

Step one is to analyze the target audience and the site strategy. I personally begin everything by sketching down ideas and designs on paper. Some people head straight to the computers, but I feel that freehand drawing is much less constrained than any computer program.

What do you think is next for Flash navigation? What improvements do you think can be made in the way Flash designers build navigation systems?

Analysis and thought. Strategy. Intuitiveness. Listening to what usability experts have to say, and applying it, not just complying blindly.

Different Navigation Design Styles and Trends

In the next sections, we review some sites to learn from real-world problems encountered by many Flash developers. In each case, we give a general summary of the project and discuss how well the site survived a usability review.

Airgid.com 2000

Airgid.com 2000, at http://www.airgid.com/2000/, represents a freelance portfolio created two years ago (see Figure 4-6). We use this example because it contains many usability mistakes many Flash developers are repeating today. This is an excellent example of how we've learned through experience to make usability a priority with design.

This site started with design as the most important goal of the project; usability wasn't explored until after many users found difficulty navigating the content. The site is contained in one pop-up window, removing all navigation elements, such as basic browser navigation, for example, Back and Forward buttons. This pop-up window was necessary because the site couldn't function properly if the Back button was present. If users clicked the Back button, they would be thrown out of the site altogether, instead of going back in the browser history, as with other web sites. A pop-up window was also created for aesthetic reasons; once again, design took preference over usability, not a good idea. When the user arrives at the final

FIGURE 4-6

Airgid.com 2000 main page

screen, four gray boxes are on the screen. No labels are associated with the boxes to give the user a clue that these are buttons. There isn't even a help system to prompt the user to explore the gray areas.

Another problem with this site is its use of inconsistent navigation. The services area (see Figure 4-7) has a totally different navigation system from the main screen. The user must relearn a new system for navigating the content. This screen also forces the user to endure animation sequences before each content area, which increases the delay in receiving the content. These animation sequences would add to users' annoyance while they're trying to obtain information.

Airgid.com 2000 Hidden Navigation

Even though this site was a good piece of art, it wasn't easy to use. When I submitted this site to the VP of a large Internet development firm, he was excited to see my new Flash creation. He entered the URL and launched the site. Later that day, I got an e-mail from him stating he liked the image, but didn't understand what the fuss was about. I asked him what he thought of my portfolio and he responded, what portfolio? Later, after more questioning, I discovered he didn't know to click on the gray buttons to continue into the rest of the site to review my portfolio. He thought the gray buttons were part of the design. Imagine if you were applying for a job and the end user couldn't navigate your content because of such a simple problem. Good navigation can make the difference between keeping your users and losing them.

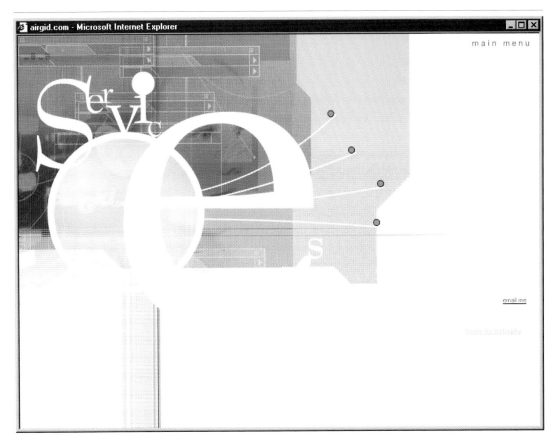

FIGURE 4-7

Airgid.com 2000 services area

The portfolio area of the site (see Figure 4-8) is the hardest to use. The images scan by at a rapid pace. The user must learn how to slow down the images by moving the cursor horizontally. No instructions are provided on how to operate this navigation system. Users must learn by trial and error to find the portfolio items in this movie. And, there's no indication that users need to click the image to obtain a larger view. Only after the users move their cursor over the image is some type of help given.

Another problem with the portfolio area is every time the user clicks to see an enlarged picture, a pop-up window is created. If the user clicks the main window, the secondary pop-up window will be pushed behind, hiding it. If the user proceeds to click open another pop-up window, the older window simply refreshes behind the main window. To the user, it appears as if nothing has happened. This problem can be solved by not

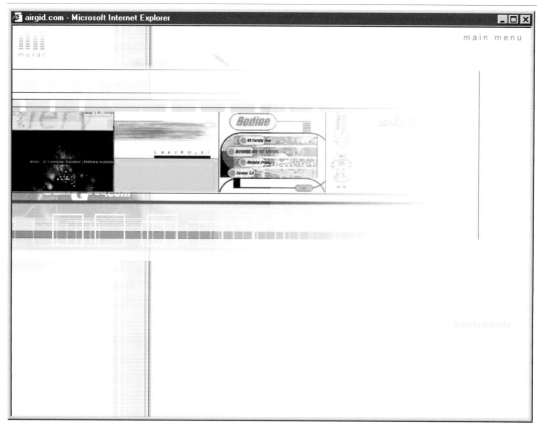

FIGURE 4-8

Airgid.com 2000 portfolio area

using pop-up windows or by loading new movies into layers in the Flash movie. Another technique to solve this problem is by including JavaScript that forces the user to close the pop-up window before they can use any other windows. A good source to find this type of JavaScript and other scripts is at http://javascript.internet.com/.

Airgid.com Overview

❯ Browser navigation, including the Back button, is not available to the user.

❯ Navigation is hidden and not completely obvious on the home page.

❯ Hidden navigation is difficult to learn because it forces users to remember what link is represented by each square.

❯ Subnavigation is inconsistent. The function and format of the navigation on each page is different, requiring users to relearn the navigation on every page as they move throughout the site.

❯ Local navigation in the portfolio section is constantly moving, which means users have to chase down the links and figure out how to move their mouse to "control" the movement. Users might also be unable to get a good idea of how many options are available in this section because the links are constantly moving back and forth.

Ultrashock.com

Ultrashock.com, at http://www.ultrashock.com/, is a resource for Flash developers who want to learn new ActionScript techniques and how to build better Flash content (see Figure 4-9). The site features an excellent, straightforward navigation system that provides ease of entry and access to valuable information. Flash content is integrated seamlessly with frames and HTML in such a way that the user has very little visual evidence of where Flash content ends and HTML begins. By blending the design of the traditional HTML with Flash, the site gains many usability functions such as the browser's Back button (see Figure 4-10). The Flash content is broken up into components and embedded on separate pages. As users move through content on the site, the browser has the opportunity to build up a history in the browser cache. When the user clicks the Back button, the web site will move back in the history, but because of the use of frames, only the center portion of the site refreshes and leaves the Flash navigation bar always visible at the top of the screen.

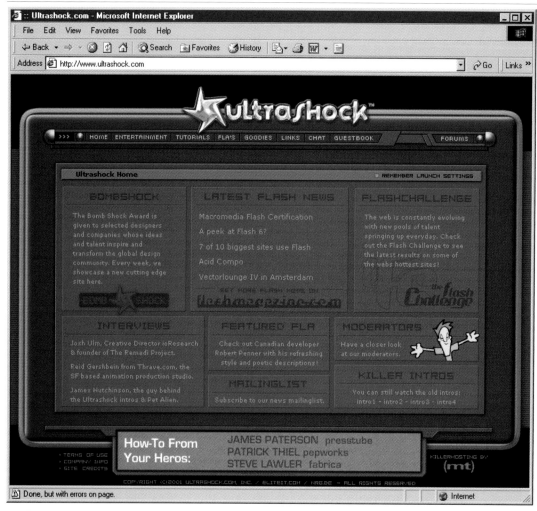

FIGURE 4-9

Ultrashock.com home page

Ultrashock.com Overview

❭ Navigation is traceable.

» Breadcrumbs are used to show a user's location within the site's information hierarchy on each page.

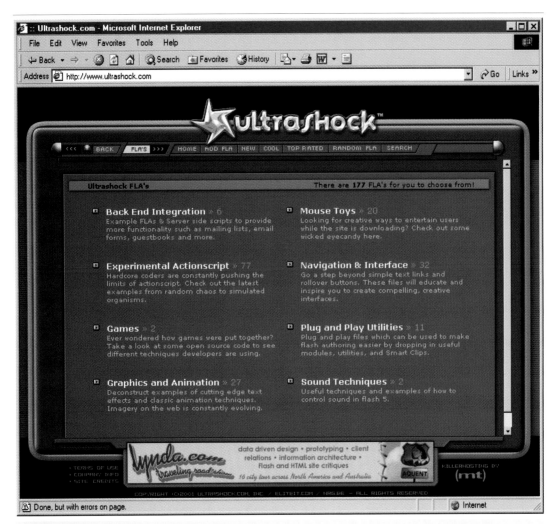

FIGURE 4-10

Ultrashock.com secondary page showing the Back button

» Graphic elements are used in the main navigation to indicate which navigation category the user is currently visiting.

» Browser Back button has been enabled to effectively give users the capability to return to the previously visited page(s).

» Additional Back button is built into Flash menu.

» The primary navigation becomes concealed when a user selects a navigation link, but a Back button is included on the navigation bar to provide users with an easy and direct means of getting back to the main navigation.

❱ Navigation is easy to learn and easy to locate.

» The main navigation bar across the top of the screen is easily recognizable as the primary navigation.

» Selecting any element from the primary navigation causes the same effect on the primary navigation bar. The nonselected labels are concealed, the selected label moves to the far right, and all subnavigation labels are displayed to the left.

❱ Navigation is consistent in its location, look, and functionality.

❱ Navigation design is excellent—it's difficult to detect where the Flash menu system ends and the traditional HTML begins.

❱ Navigation labels are descriptive of the content they represent, and appropriate for the target audience.

❱ Outside web sites to which the site links are displayed in a separated browser window to avoid "losing" the user in another site.

Peter Grafik.com

This site, at http://www.petergrafik.dk/dubonet_retro_experience/, is easy to use because navigation is big and bold and leaves nothing to chance (see Figure 4-11). Users are presented with big and clear options of well-designed icons that fit the style of the site and offer instant feedback when clicked. Because the site uses a lot of vector artwork, the download time is fast and response times are very good. Navigation elements are well labeled and easy to read, and the addition of visual references, such as icons on the buttons, helps users learn how to navigate through text and shapes. The more information you can use to help describe navigation, the better it will help users surf through your content with ease.

PeterGrafik Overview

❱ Navigation is traceable.

» The primary navigation text label remains displayed while the user navigates within that section.

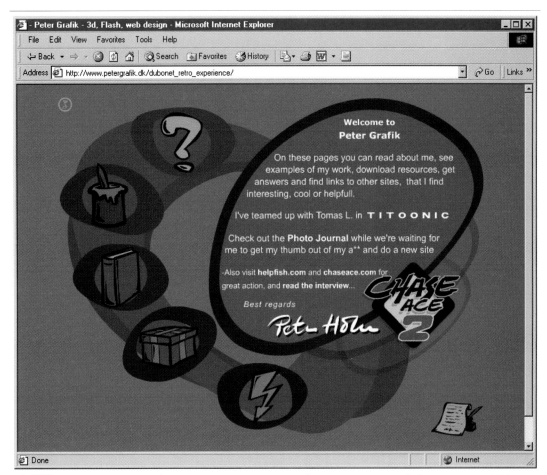

FIGURE 4-11

Petergrafik.dk

» Local navigation content populates the main display area and available subnavigation links remain visible while the user navigates within a primary section of the site.

❱ Navigation is easy to locate.

» The primary navigation icons are large and prominent on the page.

» Navigation icons are well designed and fit the style of the site.

❱ Navigation is easy to learn.

» Click and view—a simple and easy-to-use system.

❯ Primary navigation labels are descriptive of the content they represent.

❯ Label icons are supported with text labels to clarify the meaning of each and to avoid confusion and misinterpretation of the images.

Summary

Even the best possible site design can't make up for a poorly constructed navigation scheme. A well-designed navigation scheme is crucial to the success of a web site. Without it, users will be left wondering, "Where am I?" "Where do I go now?" and "How do I get there?"

Good navigation is mostly a matter of common sense, and although navigation systems will vary from site to site, usable systems tend to follow similar guidelines. In this chapter, we provided you with some of those guidelines. We've shown you some examples of Flash being used to enhance navigational usability, as well as examples of Flash being misused, such that it hinders navigation. Take this opportunity to learn from the mistakes of others and you'll avoid making the same mistakes yourself. In the next chapter, we focus on how Flash can effectively be incorporated into the content to which your users are navigating to maintain usability and continue promoting a positive experience.

Flash Usability Fast Facts

❯ A usable navigation scheme is one that's recognizable, learnable, consistent, and traceable.

❯ Make sure the labels you choose are descriptive and self-explanatory to avoid misinterpretation among different users.

❯ Iconic labels can easily be misinterpreted. Use images that are easily identifiable to all users and augment labeling icons with a text label to clarify the meaning.

❯ Flash can be used to provide a demonstration of how to use a nonstandard navigation system.

❭ Don't break the Back button on the browser. Do a little work up front and try using Robert Penner's Back button scripting example to make Flash use the browser Back button. You can find the source files for this Back button at http://www.robertpenner.com.

❭ Write down your site rules before you begin to design. Keep your site goals and target audience in mind as you lay out the navigation.

❭ Make the hit zone on your buttons larger, so it's easy for users to click the button.

❭ Try to avoid pixel fonts for navigation text because they're hard to read.

chapter **5**

Good Content Design: Ahhh, That Creamy Filling!

In the previous chapter, you learned about the importance of a site's navigation system and the ways in which Flash can positively or negatively impact usability. A site's navigation system enables the user to access every piece of content within that site, but the importance of usability doesn't end with the navigation system. Usability guidelines must carry throughout and inhabit each element on the site. In this chapter, you learn about some common characteristics of interactive content, particularly those most closely related to Flash design. You look at some of the common usability problems associated with Flash content, as well as some instances in which Flash can enhance the usability of web site content. The objective is to help you understand the importance of continually keeping your users at the forefront of your mind as you design and develop your site, particularly in instances when the design uses Flash.

Types of Content

One of the many benefits of using Flash to develop a web site is the control the developer has over content. Content such as raster images, text, and animation is easy to produce, and the resulting file sizes are much lower than most other media for the Web. By using Flash, developers can reduce the overtime it takes to produce content for a web site. Laying out complex content designs is much less time-consuming in Flash versus slicing images, exporting GIFs or JPEGs, and then adjusting tables in HTML. Once you design a layout in Flash, you can rest assured that the layout will redraw properly on more computers than it would have with standard HTML.

Graphics and Images

One of the excellent qualities of Flash is the support of PNG files. The *PNG* file format supports transparent backgrounds, much like a transparent GIF. The big difference is that PNG file transparency behaves like the "blue screening" of your local meteorologist on the news. You can export a PNG file from Photoshop with a transparent background and all the layers will retain anti-aliasing. This leaves Flash designers with the capability to use highly complex and layered designs in their Flash movies.

Using HTML, designers are limited to transparent GIF files. The problem with transparent GIF files is they are limited to on or off pixel combinations for the background that's transparent. Designers can't have smooth or faded edges with their transparent graphics. Designers can use PNG files (see Figure 5-1) in Flash to create faded edges around images and other objects. Using the PNG file format in Flash, designers can create highly layered designs, as shown in Figure 5-2.

FIGURE 5-1

This is the Save For Web export dialog box of a PNG file being exported from Adobe Photoshop 6.0

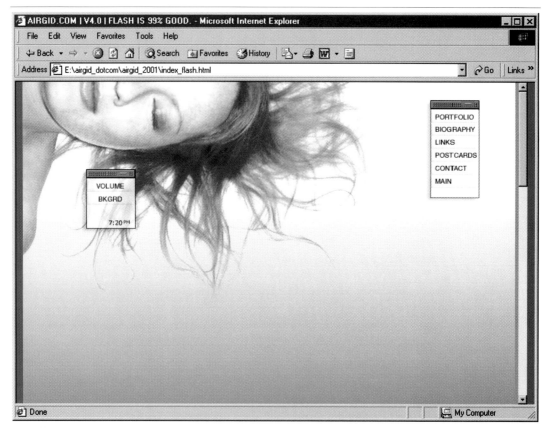

FIGURE 5-2

How the final image of the woman looks when it's imported into the Flash web site

One of the drawbacks to using raster, or bitmap, artwork in Flash is the lack of browser integration with the download process. Traditional HTML files do a better job of streaming page content down to the end user. Images can be viewed before they're completely downloaded, so users get a faster response at previewing content. Although Flash offers streaming capabilities, it doesn't enable developers to display raster images before they're downloaded. Users must wait for the whole bitmap image to download before it's displayed. Text, sound, and vector animation can stream in pieces, but bitmap images can't be partially displayed. This is a drawback if your site is bitmap-intensive. You might consider removing the bitmap images from the Flash movie, and then displaying them as pop-up windows by calling JavaScript from the Flash movie. You might consider using pop-up windows to display your bitmap images if you're creating a photo gallery or some other bitmap-intensive content. Another interesting trick to solve this problem is to create *proxy* images, or low-resolution preview images, in layers above the full-size raster image. You can set Flash to stream the content in by starting at the top layer and working down. By placing a duplicate low-resolution, highly compressed image above the full image, you give users a preview of the full graphic before it downloads. Although this adds more bytes to the file size (and it slows the download), it gives the end user the illusion that the file is downloading faster because the Flash movie will appear more responsive.

Streaming is one of the features Flash does well with symbols other than raster images. Vector symbols, animation, and sound stream effectively from Flash. By using the Bandwidth Profiler (see Figure 5-3) and testing your movie using a dial-up connection, you can build Flash content that requires no "Loading, Please Wait" movie to be played. You can give your users faster access to content as it becomes available.

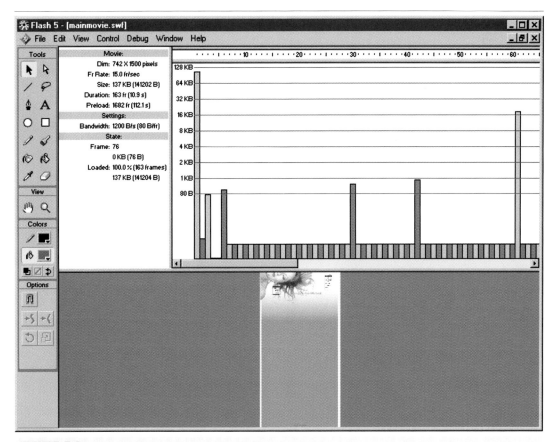

FIGURE 5-3

Example of what the Bandwidth Profiler looks like in Flash 5

One often-used technique to help offset the loading of larger content is to create a diversion. This *diversion* is something to occupy the user just long enough for you to load your Flash content in the background. Good diversions are things such as multiple-choice games that require simple text and a short ActionScript to be downloaded first. Vector animation demonstrating some type of useful information to prepare users for what's coming is another good diversion. Remember, it's important your diversion isn't only some type of eye candy. Simply having a rotating 3-D cube doesn't help. Try to build your diversion so it adds value to the content you're about to display. If you were building a Flash site for a children's cartoon series, you might consider building a small game to introduce users to the cartoon characters while the site content is loading.

Text and Typography

Typography is a powerful tool in the designer's arsenal. One of the first things designers do when they start building Flash sites is to experiment with different fonts for the body copy of the content. After being limited to Arial, Verdana, Times, or Courier in traditional HTML, designers feel that having unique fonts in Flash movies enhances their design; however, Flash designers often don't take usability into consideration when selecting typography. Many young and talented designers choose fonts that conform to current typography trends, but don't necessarily advance readability. Designers typically use high-end monitors and typography displayed on this hardware is always easy to read, so it's important to review your type choices on lower-end monitors.

Flash developers need to be sensitive to typography in their design. Using readable type can make the difference between a successful Flash site and one that flops. Designers often use pixel fonts as the main type for the body copy of the Flash movie. Pixel fonts are trendy, but they don't make a site easy to read. Pixel fonts that force all characters to uppercase are particularly hard to read because all the characters begin to look the same. To add insult to injury, when pixel fonts are set to anti-alias in the final web site, they're even harder to read. Pixel fonts aren't in themselves unusable or hard to read, it's how they're used that creates the problem. Pixel fonts are good for short titles or for type that is part of a design, or for type that serves both as design and text. Using pixel fonts for body copy that contains paragraphs of text usually isn't a good idea (see Figure 5-4).

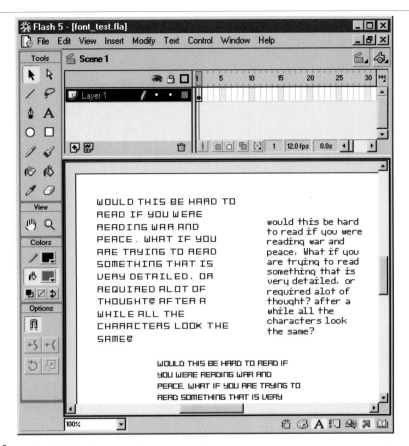

FIGURE 5-4

Non-anti-alias pixel fonts in Flash

The size of type matters greatly for type to be readable. When creating your Flash site, test your movie on your target monitor resolution (see Figure 5-5). How does the type stand up? Is it easy to read or do you need to move closer to read it comfortably?

Another consideration when choosing the type for your Flash site is the background behind the text. Try not to design images that are too

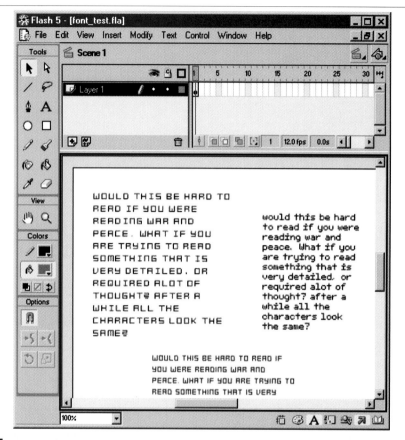

FIGURE 5-5

Example of pixel fonts in Flash with anti-alias

distracting when viewed behind large areas of text (see Figure 5-6). Solid color areas that sharply contrast the text can help make reading easier (see Figure 5-7). Black text on a gray or white background is the best and easiest way to ensure text is highly readable, but if you must include a transparent text box, make sure the text box screens out more than 75 percent of the background with a solid color.

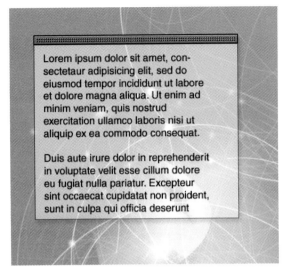

FIGURE 5-6

Text with background set to 50 percent transparency (top) and 80 percent transparency (bottom)

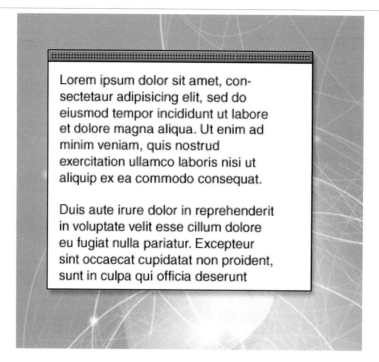

FIGURE 5-7

Text with background set to 100 percent transparency is the easiest to read

Motion and Animation

Flash started its software life as a vector animation tool. At its core, Flash has many options to let developers create cinematic experiences through the Web without the download penalty of digital video. Because of the way Flash handles resources, developers can use pieces of animation over and over for different parts of a movie to reduce file size. When creating 2-D characters in Flash, developers can break up the characters into separate symbols. For example, if you were creating a bumblebee character, you might break up the character into different parts, so you could move them independently. The head, wings, and legs would all be different symbols (see Figure 5-8).

Why You Should Consider Connecting Dual Monitors to Your Computer

Many designers who use Mac OS, Windows 98, and Windows 2000 have benefited from the capability to connect more than one monitor to the computer. Designers often have connected to the same computer a large 21-inch monitor for their work screen and a small, lower-cost 15-inch monitor as a test screen. Mac OS and certain versions of Windows have the capability to use two or more monitors to create a large desktop that can spread out between the screens. I use a large Sony Trinitron monitor as my main screen to display objects such as the Flash timeline and stage. I use my secondary 15-inch monitor to display palettes and the Actions window to keep my screen free of clutter, so I can concentrate on the Flash design. I also use the secondary monitor as a test monitor to see how type and graphics will look on a low-end monitor at a smaller resolution, such as 800×600.

You can easily set up a dual monitor system on your computer. It requires a second video card and a cheap monitor. Setting up the dual monitor is easy on the Mac OS and it isn't that hard in Windows 2000 either.

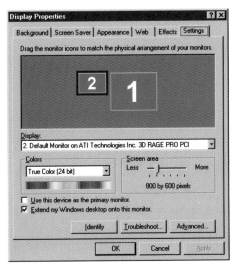

I highly recommend a dual monitor setup—the cost of a low-end monitor and video card can save you many hours in development time.   –K.A.

For more information about dual monitors, check out these sites:
http://www.geek.com/features/doublevision/
http://www.hereontheweb.com/dual/
http://freepctech.com/pc/001/guide_dual_monitors.shtml

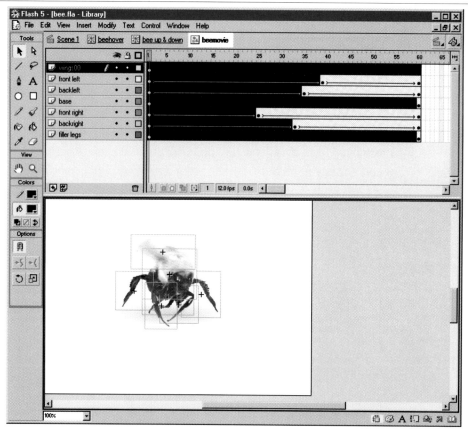

FIGURE 5-8

Example of bumblebee 2-D character broken up into different symbols in Flash

By importing each object separately and creating a different symbol for each one, you can create smaller components that can be animated within Flash. So, if you want to move the legs from top to bottom, you would simply animate the symbols and let Flash tween the in-between frames. If you wanted to accomplish this in digital video, you would need to render each frame for the in-between frames, creating a larger file size. Also, because the bumblebee is a movie, you can create multiple instances of the movie to produce a swarm of bees, and the end user would have to download only one set of resources for the wings, legs, and body. Flash's capability to reuse symbols is its most powerful feature.

Many Flash animators concentrate solely on the animation and getting it right, but give little thought to how to conserve bandwidth. Flash developers often create animations that are well designed and executed, but the file size is too large for a comfortable download even at DSL and cable modem speeds. Users are forced to endure long-loading movies. In other instances, to create a small file size, Flash developers compress the quality of the movie to such a degree the images begin to look poor. Planning your animation with your target bandwidth in mind is important.

Before you begin creating your Flash animation it's a good idea to sketch it out on paper first. Create a storyboard of your ideas before you commit to hours of developing your animation in front of Flash. As you're sketching out your ideas, think about how you can reuse images, sounds, and other pieces of your sequence to help reduce the file size. Also, remember your target audience as you develop your animation. How fast is your target audience's computer? This is an important issue because high frame rates and complex animation sequences will play sluggishly on lower-end systems. Even extremely fast computers with the latest CPU might have a slower video card than your machine, so it's important to test early and often when developing your animation. Here are a few good points to check if your movie is playing too slowly:

> Limit moving large raster images across the screen. Many medium-speed computers will begin to play sluggishly.

> If possible, avoid scaling your movie by percentage. The larger the area the computer has to refresh, the slower the animation will play.

> Try reducing your movie frame rate and reducing the distance between key frames. This will make your movie look like it's running faster.

> Avoid the use of multiple movie clips animating at the same time. This often causes delays in animation.

Personal Viewpoint
Test Early and Test Often

From experience, I can tell you if you don't test your Flash animation early and often, you won't enjoy the consequences. Two computers that are exactly the same with the same hardware, but with different operating systems, can behave in a totally different way when playing Flash movies. A good idea is to test your movie on as many types of computer systems as you can. Testing for your target audience is always the most important.

–Kevin Airgid

3-D Animation in Flash

Using vector files to create 3-D animation in Flash can produce stunning results at a low cost to file size. You can create 3-D animation in Flash with different techniques. These techniques are beyond the scope of this book, but we'll explore ways that users can apply 3-D animation to a Flash site to make it more usable.

Q & A Interview with Andries Odendaal, Wireframe Studio

Andries, can you give us some information on your background and your experience?

I'm 29 years old, and I live and work in Cape Town, South Africa, at a multimedia agency called Wireframe. I've been working in the multimedia field for about four years now, mostly on CD-ROM projects. The Net has been a more recent venture, about two years or so. I formally studied fine art (sculpture and printmaking) after which I gradually became more interested in new technologies. More recently, I've been focusing specifically on Flash development and have completed a number of web-based games and web sites in this medium.

What's the biggest challenge to Flash developers as far as usability? What do you think is the biggest mistake most users make?

The thing about Flash is that it allows almost total freedom in designing user interfaces. However, considering the short turnaround time allocated for many web projects, it becomes difficult to manage this freedom. Many Flash projects are not completed to the state that I would prefer and, as a result, this often impacts on usability. If I have one criticism, it would be about the time spent "finishing" or fine-tuning projects. For instance, people reinvent scroll bars in Flash, and then don't bother about the finer details. My pet peeve is Flash scroll bars that scroll anti-aliased text at two frames a second. For something to be usable, it should not only be at the right place at the right time. It should also be responsive ... a big mistake is to develop on a high-spec machine.

Describe the process you go through to ensure that Flash sites work on the computer of your target audience. How do you test to ensure the Flash site works properly at the end of the project?

Well, first of all, the great thing about Flash is it's cross-platform-compatible, so this already helps to ensure things will work on most of the computers of the target audience. Testing usually happens by sending some friends and colleagues the link and asking them to test it. We have both Macs and PCs in the studio and we usually try to test things on the various platforms, especially on low-end machines. Different projects obviously do have different minimum requirements and we test accordingly. We've had some larger projects before where we got together user focus groups to test the products.

Our bandwidth on this side of the world also leaves much to be desired, which has been working as an advantage because we know what it's like to wait. So download times are a big concern here, to we try and design accordingly.

Has creating ActionScript-based 3-D objects in Flash enabled you to make your Flash sites more usable?

No, not in the traditional sense. I don't think that 3-D by default makes something more usable. 3-D navigation is almost always a problem and is quite ambiguous. However, I try to create more "tangible" experiences. I like the user to drag things around, and explore and play with things and manipulate them. This isn't the easiest or simplest means of navigating or experiencing a project, but I think these are "usable" features, and depending on the project, this can create a more involved experience. 3-D has been quite useful in this because it enforces the illusion of the tangible.

When you build advanced 3-D objects using ActionScript in Flash, do you ever have to worry about the end user's computer being too slow to render the objects? And, if so, how do you solve this problem?

Yes, this is a concern and this is generally a concern with most heavy ActionScript applications. I've never been a fan of smoothly rendered 3-D. What intrigues me is the 3-D motion and the capability to manipulate "objects" in real time. To this end, I've been keeping the 3-D objects simple and light, which creates its own aesthetic. The low-quality feature in Flash is also something that's underused and speeds things up considerably.

How do you judge if a Flash site is successful from a usability standpoint?

I think usability is probably the most important feature of a site, and that includes interface, bandwidth constraints, and so forth. I don't think intuitive interface design necessarily means either boring interface design or well-established methods of navigation. I do think there's merit in challenging the user but, to be intuitive, it has to make sense.

But there's another side to usability I often look for, and I always have trouble expressing this. I see interaction as having an almost "tangible" property and I believe there's a lot to be learned from games in this regard. It's nested in the subtleties and I think Pacman is a good example in that, when you run into one of the "ghosts," the hit test doesn't register a hit until the main character and the ghost overlap about halfway. I doubt that the game would have had the same level of playability if it wasn't for this subtle feature. It allows for human error and lends a pleasant "softness" (for the lack of a better word) to the game. It's something you can feel without necessarily being aware of—you can feel it in your bones. It's almost tangible. I'm sorry if this sounds a bit obscure but, for me, this forms a large part of usability.

So, beyond primary functionality, elements within a user interface system also communicate via their own properties (color, motion, responsiveness, and so forth); even underlined HTML links have a particular, almost "tactile" quality, which results in a particular human experience when being clicked. I believe that attention to these kinds of details can communicate an idea/philosophy in a different way than the written word can and, in doing so, these details become not only usability features, but also communication devices.

Flash enables us to create these custom usability features. It lets you choose the hit area, the size of a button, or the responsiveness or color of an object, and it's up to the developer to consider how all these things can impact usability. This is liberating for a developer, but it has its pitfalls if the developer isn't willing to invest time in these details. For me, usability lies in the subtleties.

What mistakes have you made in the past regarding Flash usability? And how did you resolve them?

I've made many mistakes in the past and I still do. I think we still have a lot to learn about the medium, and most of the time I experiment with alternative ideas, rather than following a clear usability model. With this approach, you're bound to make mistakes, but in the long run, I think you learn a lot more about usability and the potential of breaking ground.

One thing that's been problematic for me is the way many of us are guilty, especially on the Web, in our approach to building projects. Most of the time we seem to be building containers for information, rather than building effective multimedia. Most of the time it's about the content (which is usually in text form), and then solving the problem of how to get to it/structure it. I think that multimedia is more conducive to being the content than being the container.

As long as you see the content of a site as separate from the navigation or multimedia elements, I think you will always have usability issues. Many of my projects have been quite "usable" in the sense that there are things to play with and it's quite fun to interact with, but it fails as navigation, which it has been partly created for. An example is http://www.wireframe.co.za/com-ebusiness—a fun interface that will probably keep you busy for a while, but not a great way of navigating and the important content (the copy, information) is a bit of an anticlimax. I would have felt better if the content were more integrated; if the onscreen activity itself could communicate the full message in a playful manner, rather than be a means of getting to the content.

Flash developers, such as Wireframe Studio (http://www.wireframe.co.za/), harness advanced ActionScript to create real gravity and three-dimensional properties dynamically in Flash. Many of the 3-D examples Wireframe displays on its site are generated using math-heavy ActionScripts to calculate inertia and draw vector objects in a 3-D space (see Figure 5-9).

This method is excellent because it reduces the file size of the Flash movie to only a few symbols. The downloaded symbols are then manipulated using ActionScript to create a 3-D effect. In most cases, downloading the calculations of 3-D objects is an excellent method to reduce file size and to create better interactivity (see Figure 5-10). Because the objects are drawn in a 3-D space by ActionScript, the developer can create more complex animation that can respond to user input. The drawback to downloading the rendering of the vector objects is the concern that the end user's computer might be too slow to draw the objects properly. Once again, testing your movie on your target audience machine is important. Although ActionScripts don't generally consume a lot of CPU resources, math-heavy functions, such as custom 3-D scenes, might increase the use of system resources.

When to Use Motion and Animation in Flash

Everyone has heard the saying "a picture is worth a thousand words." Most animation says *millions* of words. Animation is sometimes the most effective tool Flash developers can use to convey a hard-to-describe service or educational material. For example, Flash animation can be used to provide a virtual product demonstration, such as how to operate a cellular phone. The site might walk the user through each function of the phone with an interactive menu. A hand could appear to punch the correct keys on the

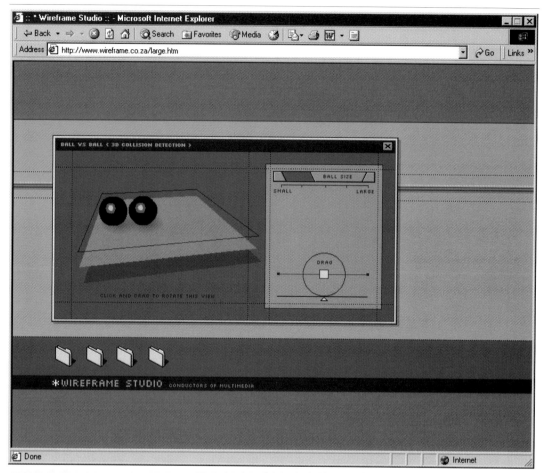

FIGURE 5-9

Ball vs. Ball (3-D Collision Detection) from wireframe.co.za

phone to demonstrate a function of the phone. The user learns how the phone operates through sight and sound, and by reading the instructions. This way, the Flash module engages several of your senses to help educate you on the product.

Flash animation is also an effective method to grab users' attention, such as when it's used in banner advertising. Flash banner ads can contain more detailed and longer animation than a traditional animated GIF, but without increased file sizes. The more interesting the banner, the more likely the target audience might click and interact with it. Flash animation also can be combined with interactivity to create a *smart* banner ad. This smart

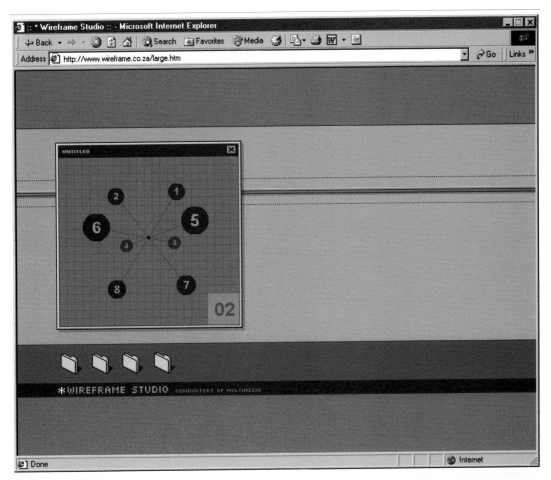

FIGURE 5-10

Untitled example from wireframe.co.za

Flash banner can be self-contained and require no link to an external site. Features such as the capability to print a coupon directly from the Flash banner can help increase the use of such advertising media. For example, Flash developers can create a movie that plays when the banner loads. The movie can contain an internal symbol that, when called on, can be printed directly to the end user's printer. Flash banner ads can also contain sound, something traditional banner ads could never do. We strongly recommend you don't use sound in your Flash banner ads unless your target audience will accept this. Nothing is worse than making your target audience angry with advertising that breaks into the playback of their favorite MP3.

During the launch of Windows XP, Microsoft used Flash banner ads that contained animation and sound. These banner ads were well integrated into the content of sites. Using a new technique of embedding Flash 5 in a DHTML layer, the Flash developers created a Flash movie that could expand over the content. (A good place to find a tutorial on how to embed Flash 5 content in DHTML layers is on the Flash Kit web site at http://www.flashkit.com/tutorials/index.shtml.) This gave the Flash banner ad the capability to grow when the user wanted to play the animation contained in the ad. This technique could only be viewed by users who had the Flash 5 plug-in and Internet Explorer 4 and above. This technology limit was acceptable because the target audience primarily had this browser configuration. Users surfing and using the Mac OS were probably not interested in upgrading to Windows XP, so the use of this specific plug-in and browser version was justified.

Flash as a Major Movie Experience

Flash has grown from small intro movies to epic theatrical online events. Many sites now feature full-length cartoon adventures each week. Macromedia's Shockwave.com (http://www.shockwave.com/) features full-animation episodes of various short films and cartoons. Users can return each week to see new episodes, making the web experience more like television. Although Flash has a compressed file time, full-screen movielike experiences within Flash are still for users with broadband connections and faster computers.

By displaying the Flash movie in full-screen mode using Internet Explorer's Full Screen command, Flash developers can remove the gray browser window and transport users to an experience more like television. Make certain you warn your users before you switch to full screen and always provide a way to close the full-screen mode by applying an obvious Close or Quit button, or a link with a message "This will now launch your browser into full-screen mode." Although taking over the user's screen might be appropriate for your cinematic movie, users won't appreciate having their screen hijacked without a choice. Always include a button. Also, it's important not to place your whole site into full-screen mode. By removing the browser interface elements, such as Back and Forward buttons, you reduce your site's usability.

When you launch your movie into full-screen mode, make sure to test your movie out on many platforms. Netscape Navigator doesn't respond to full-screen commands the way Internet Explorer does, so you need to be cautious and test your scripts on many platforms when you develop your movie this way.

Q & A Interview with Toke Nygaard and Michael Schmidt, Creators of KALIBER10000

Background information:

Toke Nygaard Born 1973 in Denmark; atttended The Danish School of Design; art director at Araneum, Copenhagen 97–99; art director at Oven Digital, London 99–01; currently working at Wallpaper* magazine; founding member of The Embassy of Code and Form; cofounder of KALIBER10000.

Michael Schmidt Born 1974 in Denmark; attended The University of Copenhagen; freelanced for various ad agencies, Copenhagen 95–96; art director at On-line magazine, Copenhagen 96–97; art director at Adcore DBC, Copenhagen 97–00; creative director at Adcore Ltd., London 00–01; currently freelancing in San Francisco; cofounder of KALIBER10000.

As the curators of KALIBER10000 (http://www.k10k.net/), what Flash contributions to your portal stand out as good examples of effective animation?

- Issue 025 Ottergirl—sweet story, good sound, nice animation
- Issue 017 Garden—insane nonsense animation
- Issue 047 Four Winds—beautiful and quiet, atmospheric setting
- Issue 067 Empty City—captures the essence of the modern city
- Issue 079 Noizes and Spikes (Shockwave)—one of our first sound issues
- Issue 084 Transit.7—a bandwidth-heavy crazy mixture of Flash and QuickTime
- Issue 085 722—Flash animation in its purest, most geometrical form
- Issue 087 Client-o-matic—fun and pretty accurate
- Issue 088 Powers that Lurk—more insane nonsense animation
- Issue 110 The Slide-box—one of our favorite issues, intricate and innovative, and a ton more. Almost all our recent issues have used Flash as their technology of choice—and a lot of them have been truly stunning examples of well-crafted Flash animation.

What Flash sites do you think are the most usable and why?

Toke: None. The Flash-driven sites I like are mostly cartoony sites and they're not really usable.

Michael: Web sites that use individual Flash elements for specific functions—like a menu, a display system, or a shopping cart. In those areas, Flash really shines and can be used for something quite extraordinary. Off the top of my head, however, I can't recall having seen any Flash sites recently that were good examples of usability—but then, most Flash sites seem to focus on the animation capabilities of the program, on creating lovely intro screens, smoothly fading menu systems, and so forth.

What would be your best advice for designers who want to build creative, yet usable, Flash sites?

Toke: Keep trying. Keep your eyes open. Draw inspiration and knowledge from real old-school use of animation and sound. Keep exploring. If Flash doesn't do the trick, look elsewhere for other ways of doing it. Is there an idea behind what you're doing?

Michael: If you're serious about usability in Flash, you can't just create a web site that's one huge Flash file—by doing so you remove many top-level functions that have been built into the browser, such as the Back and Forward buttons, and so forth, and also effectively limit the users' capability to control their browser environment. So, until Macromedia finds a way to better integrate Flash elements in browsers, instead of merely layering them on top of everything, I'd stick to creating specific Flash elements and integrating them into the rest of the web site.

Content Placement

Content placement is one of the most important issues when laying out Flash content, and it can make the difference between a site that's easy to use and one that isn't. Placing important content where it can be retrieved quickly sounds like an obvious decision, but many Flash developers conceal important content in either hard-to-navigate custom-interface elements or secondary movies. It is critical to research your target audience with much energy and attention. Try to get into their mindset. What types of information are most important to them? Making users sit through introduction movies without a Skip button is a small example of how to turn your Flash site experience into a negative one—especially if users want to get at information quickly.

In newspapers, things that are extremely important, such as navigational elements, are always "above the fold" on the front page. When developing Flash sites, the fold is where the page disappears off the screen on a conventional page that has scrolling. Many Flash developers create content that doesn't scroll within the browser window, but is contained solely within the Flash movie. Regardless of whether the movie scrolls in the browser or has custom scroll devices within the Flash movie, developers must be sensitive to the placement of content.

Try to place the most important content either on the entry page or no more than one click deep. The information should be clearly labeled and obvious. For instance, if you were creating a Flash site for a company that sells rare coins, you might consider placing the most sought-after coins on the entry page to the site. Because the users' main goal is to browse and purchase coins, they probably don't want to wade through other information to get at their objective.

Screen resolution also affects content placement because it can determine how your Flash design is displayed. If you're creating content that primarily contains vector objects, you might consider scaling your movies by percentage. This will enable your content to scale to the appropriate size of the monitor's resolution. This is one of Flash's unique qualities, but it's not without drawbacks. If you scale your movies by percentage, you must be aware that slower computers will have trouble playing back animations that are larger. If your movie consumes the whole screen, the animations might play slower on lower-end computers. Also, if your movies contain raster (bitmap) images, the quality of such images will be reduced when they scale beyond their original size. Setting your movie to a fixed width and height by pixels is good if you want to display many raster images and animation. This way, you can control the area that will be animated. Setting your movies by pixels is also effective because you can ensure that type doesn't expand into huge clunky blocks on higher-resolution computers.

Bookmarking Content

Virtually every Internet user is familiar with the practice of bookmarking a site they want to return to easily without typing in a URL. Bookmarks are used by approximately 84 percent of users to revisit favorite sites, according to a survey conducted by Georgia Tech's GVU (Graphics, Visualization, and Usability) center. Another study found that over 34 percent of users have at least 100 URLs bookmarked and only 2 percent of users have never bookmarked a site. Most users know if they want to get back to a site quickly and easily, they should bookmark it. When a user decides to bookmark your site, consider it a compliment. They've just told you they value your site enough to make sure they're able to return. In most cases, this means they've enjoyed a positive experience while using your site.

Unfortunately, a common problem with many Flash sites and Flash content within sites is the difficulty that arises when trying to use the browser's Bookmark feature (also known as Favorites). In some instances, designers eliminate the URL entirely by disabling the browser's toolbar in the window that displays the Flash content. As a general rule, this is never a wise decision. Eliminating the browser toolbar eliminates the users' most familiar and well-understood means of managing the display within their browser window. Most users are unaware of and unfamiliar with using alternative methods, such as keyboard commands and the right-mouse click, that can be used to accomplish some, but not all, of the major toolbar functions. And, in most cases, these shortcuts won't work within the Flash environment.

In other instances, the browser's toolbar is left completely intact; however, the Flash site or content is imbedded within one single HTML page. Choosing to bookmark will only bookmark the HTML page that contains the Flash movie, but won't enable a user to save the location of specific content within the Flash movie. When a user returns to that bookmarked URL, they won't see the piece of content they thought they bookmarked. Instead, they'll have to navigate back to it from the HTML page that was bookmarked. Depending on the type of content being bookmarked, this might be a fairly simple task or it might be time-consuming and complex.

As a designer, this might not seem like a big deal, especially while you're engulfed in the creative process. What's a few extra mouse clicks or a few extra seconds spent searching to a user anyway? After all, the mere fact that Flash content can't be bookmarked doesn't mean the site is completely unusable, does it? Of course not. Your site might, in every other way, provide a positive online experience for your users. In fact, if it hasn't, then chances are you won't have to worry about this because you won't have any users who want to bookmark your site. After all, how many users want to return to a site that leaves them frustrated, confused, and unable to accomplish the goals they came to fulfill? Not many (perhaps that's why Internet Explorer labels this feature Favorites).

Recall in Chapter 2, we discussed the importance of attracting, engaging, and retaining your users. Chances are, if your site has made it to the point of being considered a favorite in a user's mind, then you've done at least a few things right (from both a design and a usability perspective). They're attracted. They're engaged. Now you simply have to retain them—you have to keep them coming back. Retaining your users means not only making sure they'll want to return, but also that they can. Sure, there are other avenues to find a site you liked besides bookmarks, such as the most popular search engines. But those few extra seconds searching for your site on Yahoo! or Google will probably provide your users with a number of search results besides your site and could drop them right into the hands of your competition.

So what's a Flash designer to do? At a minimum, avoid the practice of disabling the browser's toolbar in the window that displays the Flash content. With this toolbar intact, users at least have the capability to bookmark the page that lets them get to the Flash content they want, which is better than nothing. Without at least the minimum functionality of the toolbar available, many users have no means whatsoever of making sure they can return to your site or the content within it. Next, look at the navigation system and the process a user must go through to get to a specific piece of content (specifically, the Flash content). Is it a fairly horizontal structure that requires only one or two clicks to get to the deepest level of content? Or, is it a content-intensive site that requires a more vertical navigation structure to get to the deeper levels of content? If it's the latter, then you might want to consider breaking up the Flash movie into segments that can be distributed across several web pages, which can then be individually bookmarked. The time and effort required to design Flash content in this manner is minimal compared to the time and effort required for a user to find that content again without a straightforward bookmarking technique.

To summarize, here are some Flash content bookmarking guidelines:

> Avoid eliminating the address bar in the browser window that displays the site's URL.

> Avoid eliminating the browser toolbar, which contains key browser navigation tools, including the one used for bookmarking.

> In instances where the content on the site is organized using a vertical navigation structure, consider breaking up the content in the Flash movie into segments that can be individually bookmarked.

Printing Flash Content

Another commonly cited problem with Flash is the difficulty or inability to print the content within the Flash movie. It's interesting to note here that many of the problems (including printing problems) users experience with Flash content aren't a result of some weakness associated with the Flash software. Flash is an inherently beneficial design tool that provides designers with the capability to create unique functionality to improve usability and enhance the user experience. As with any tool, however, Flash must be used intelligently and appropriately. If you used a chainsaw to cut a sandwich, you'd end up with a mess. Although a chainsaw is a powerful cutting tool, it wasn't designed or intended to be used on sandwiches. Is the mess you ended up with the result of a problem with the chainsaw? No—it's a problem with the way the chainsaw was applied.

Common Flash Printing Problems

One of the most common errors made by designers when designing a site in Flash is placing text in a small box with a scroll bar to enable the users to scroll as they read (Figure 5-11). In many cases, this text also is displayed using small, difficult-to-read fonts that don't print well. If the user decides to print the text, only the amount of text shown in the textbox will print.

Another design-related print problem occurs when the content is displayed in a narrow vertical format—the type users must scroll down the screen to read. When they try to print this content, it prints exactly as it's shown on the screen. The user inevitably ends up printing numerous pages with a two-inch wide column of text running down each page—not exactly the most efficient way to print a document and not easy to read either. In cases where you have an animated Flash presentation, printing is virtually impossible. Attempting to print the content of the presentation often yields only the first frame of the movie and nothing else.

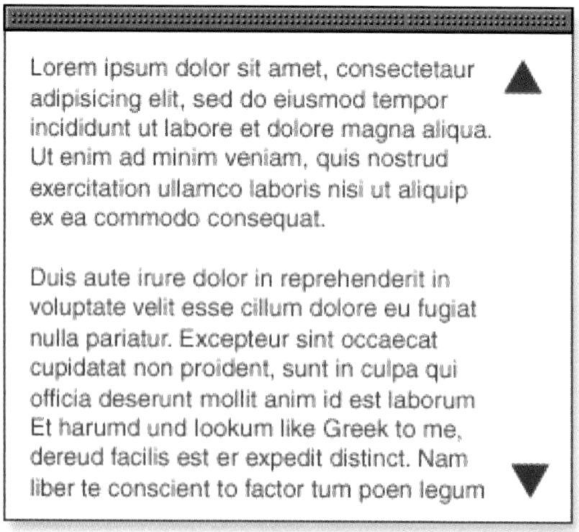

Lorem ipsum dolor sit amet, consectetaur adipisicing elit, sed do eiusmod tempor incididunt ut labore et dolore magna aliqua. Ut enim ad minim veniam, quis nostrud exercitation ullamco laboris nisi ut aliquip ex ea commodo consequat.

Duis aute irure dolor in reprehenderit in voluptate velit esse cillum dolore eu fugiat nulla pariatur. Excepteur sint occaecat cupidatat non proident, sunt in culpa qui officia deserunt mollit anim id est laborum Et harumd und lookum like Greek to me, dereud facilis est er expedit distinct. Nam liber te conscient to factor tum poen legum

FIGURE 5-11

Scrolling text is often difficult to print when placed in a small window, such as this one

Many designers seem to feel an innate need to remove the browser toolbar on the window that displays the Flash site or content. Although doing this might enhance the visual appeal of the site, it can detract greatly from the overall usability. As mentioned earlier, this toolbar is, for the most part, your users' only means of controlling their browser display. And, although you might feel the necessity of taking away that control to maintain the look and feel of your design, users often don't know what to do without it. Eliminating this toolbar means users can't access the Print function, among other things. Even if the content could be printed, many users might not know how to print in the absence of the toolbar.

Here's a quick recap of the common Flash printing problems:

❱ Text that scrolls in a small window or text box can't be printed in its entirety. Only the text shown in the window on the screen will print.

❱ Text is displayed using small, difficult-to-read fonts that don't print well.

❱ Text displayed in a narrow vertical format is inefficient to print and difficult to read once it's printed.

❱ Animated Flash presentations aren't printable—only the first frame of the movie will print.

❱ Browser toolbar is removed, eliminating the user's main access to the Print function.

Simple Flash Printing Solutions

There are ways to manage all the problems just pointed out. You should begin by leaving the browser toolbar in place. This is the best option to maximize usability. However, for those of you sitting there breaking out in hives at the very thought of this, a few exceptions to this rule can be considered. Eliminating the toolbar will trigger the fewest number of adverse usability-related consequences when the following two conditions have been met:

❱ The content within the browser window can't be printed using the browser Print function and you provided a separate Print function within your movie that's obvious and understandable to your users.

❱ You're certain the majority of your users are familiar with Flash content and will value the design-related advantages associated with removing the toolbar over and above the loss of functionality that might result.

If either of these conditions haven't been met, we strongly suggest leaving the toolbar intact.

Another way to eliminate printing problems with Flash content is to provide a printable version of the content that's been displayed in a nonprintable format. For example, if you choose to scroll paragraphs of text through a small window on the screen, provide a link to a printable version of the text. This can be done by creating an HTML or PDF version of the content. Or, if your site is offered in both Flash and HTML format, it might be helpful to remind users who choose the Flash site that a printable version of the content can be found on the HTML version of the site. A link directly to the specific section being printed is another helpful touch and saves users the trouble of having to navigate to content on the HTML site that they'd already found on the Flash version. Note, however, if you decide to do this, a good idea is to open the HTML version of the site in a new window (making it obvious to the user this is a new window). If you don't do this, your users might get confused when, once they finish printing, they try to continue navigating the site and are unable to return to the Flash version they originally chose.

To summarize, here are some simple Flash printing solutions:

❭ Leave the browser toolbar in place on the browser window.

❭ Provide a printable version of content that's been displayed on the site in an unprintable (or difficult-to-print) format.

❭ Offer users an HTML version that can easily be printed if the entire site is designed in Flash.

Does Everything Have to Be Printable?

The following is a list of the most commonly printed content types. If you're designing a site or portion of a site that falls into any of these categories, make every effort to provide users with a means of printing the content.

❭ Lists of information

❭ Company information (such as about products and services offered, company management, contact information, and so forth)

❭ Product information (such as specifications and comparisons)

❭ Educational or instructional material (such as tutorials, timelines, demonstrations, and so forth)

> ❱ Articles

> ❱ Receipts (after completing an online purchase)

> ❱ Presentations

Flash Forms

Web-based forms let users interact with a web site in a formatted fashion by inputting specific information related to the type of form being used. When used wisely, forms can be one of the most effective means of enabling your users to communicate with you. When used incorrectly, forms can be a key cause of confusion and frustration for users. Forms are used for a wide variety of purposes. Some, such as feedback forms and Contact Us forms, enable users to send questions or information (usually by e-mail) to a recipient. Forms also can be used to gather information on users through online surveys and questionnaires. When shopping on an e-commerce site, users complete their purchases by *checking out*—a process that normally entails submitting their purchase, shipping, and billing information via a form. Search systems let users search for specific content, based on criteria they input using a search form. Forms vary in length, type, format, and design, but to be effective, all forms must have one thing in common—they must be usable.

So, you might be wondering, how do I know if the form I designed is usable? In general, the guidelines for designing a usable form are the same as the guidelines discussed in Chapter 4 for creating a usable navigation and labeling system. In essence, when a user is interacting with a form, they're "navigating" through the form-filling process, selecting and inputting information before submitting the final product. The main difference between general web site navigation and navigation as it relates to the use of forms is that *form navigation* is usually a linear process. In a multistep form, while users might be allowed to jump back to a previous step in the form-filling process, they typically complete a form in a linear, step-by-step progression before finally submitting it at the end. It's important for the design of your form to facilitate this type of process.

Flash-based forms have a tendency to suffer from a number of usability-related problems. Flash-based sites often incorporate ultracreative, nonstandard design elements and, as a result, so do their forms, which can cause problems for the user. Forms require a great deal of interaction with the end user—far beyond just pointing-and-clicking in most cases. To complete a form, users must process information, come to a conclusion, and input the results of that conclusion using the form you've provided. How difficult or easy this cognitive process is on your users depends greatly on the type of form they're interacting with. In any case, though, when users are filling out forms, their brains are busy—busy enough that they don't need to be troubled with the added task of figuring out how to use your form. Give their brains a break by following a few important guidelines. Your users (and their brains) will thank you.

Guidelines to Ensure Usable Flash-Based Form Design

The usability guidelines for Flash-based forms are very closely related to the navigation guidelines we discussed in Chapter 4. To ensure usability, forms should be recognizable, learnable, and traceable.

Recognizable

One of the biggest problems with Flash forms is they aren't always easily recognizable as forms. The design of a Flash-based form often bears only minimal resemblance to the typical HTML-based web forms with which most users are familiar. Flash-based text fields, radio buttons, and check boxes look more like design elements than fields requiring user input.

The form shown in Figure 5-12 is an example of a potentially troublesome Flash form. Although the form fields are clearly labeled, it's difficult to determine where to begin typing. It appears as though the small white boxes might be a starting point, but clicking any of them fails to produce a cursor. After some further haphazard clicking around with the mouse, it becomes evident that the actual text fields begin a few spaces after the white boxes. The exception is the Message field. When the user gets to this field, more random clicking must be done to locate the cursor, which is now under the Message heading. Clicking to the right of the heading produces no cursor or results. If the user had clicked only in the area to the right of the heading—assuming the field locations were consistent—they might have given up and either left the page or sent the form without a message. Without a more familiar format or a blinking cursor in place, users might assume that either a) the form isn't a form at all and is not a means for inputting information or b) something is wrong with the form, which is why the blinking cursor is absent from the page. In either case, users might then skip, overlook, or ignore the form.

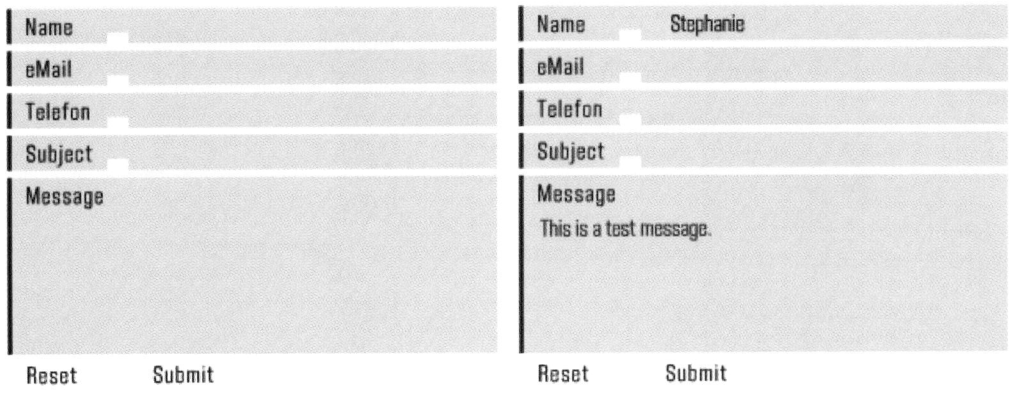

Name		Name	Stephanie
eMail		eMail	
Telefon		Telefon	
Subject		Subject	
Message		Message	
		This is a test message.	
Reset	Submit	Reset	Submit

FIGURE 5-12

The unusual design and function of this form makes it more difficult to recognize and use

Figure 5-13 shows an example of a much more usable form. Like the form in Figure 5-12, this form was created in Flash. The difference is this form incorporates some recognizable key elements, such as standard-shaped text boxes with a blinking cursor that indicates where the user should begin typing. The cursor position also remains consistent throughout the form. Small, subtle design elements such as this can make a big difference in how users react to and interact with the form you designed. Form design is one where function must take precedence over form (design)—no pun intended.

Learnable

Forms should be easy to learn. Users should be able to understand how to use a form with little cognitive effort. As mentioned earlier—your users are already putting their brains to good use by coming up with the information they need to complete the form. Learnable forms incorporate the following elements:

- An *intuitive design* that doesn't stray so far from the norm that it becomes unrecognizable as a form.

- *Descriptive labels* that provide the user with a clear definition of the information that must be provided.

- *Logical functionality* that doesn't require a separate help section for a typical user to understand. How the form works should be fairly

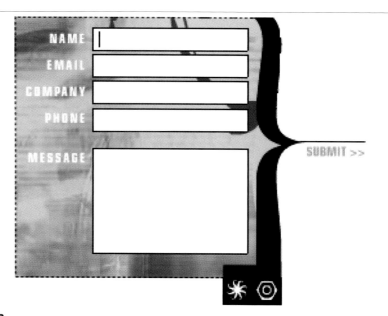

FIGURE 5-13

Elements like a blinking cursor and standard-type text boxes make this form more recognizable and easier to use

obvious. Instruction should be provided in steps or sections that require information or action that might not be obvious to the user.

One problem with Flash forms is they don't typically support the TAB key functionality the way HTML forms do. In an HTML-based form, a user can use the TAB key to move from field to field. In Flash, this functionality isn't available unless the designer builds it in. TAB key functionality is only available in Flash 5 and above. Flash 4 does enable tabbing between text fields, but the designer decides the order, based on a left-to-right, top-to-bottom order of the text fields in the movie. Depending on how your form fields are organized, this may or may not be useful. For instance, if you created a form design using Flash 4 that organizes information into multiple columns, tabbing might send your users back and forth between unrelated columns of information. In this case, incorporating a more vertical design that would enable users to tab through each form field in the correct order would be better. Leading your users through a logical succession when filling out form information is important, so you don't confuse or frustrate them in the process.

Traceable

In Chapter 4, the term "traceable" was used to describe a navigation system that provides feedback to the user as to where they are in the site and allows them to retrace navigation steps easily to a particular section of the site. For a form to be traceable, it should incorporate similar feedback and backward navigation elements. This won't apply to all forms. Some forms, such as search forms and short feedback forms, are brief and can easily be contained within one page or step. Some forms are much longer, though, and require the user to go through multiple steps or pages before submitting the form. If this is the case, a good idea is to let the users know how far along in the form-filling process they are and, in some cases, to enable them to return to a previous step or page in the process easily. For example, at each step (or page) in the form, let the users know which step they're on and how many steps remain. In situations where users might need to go back to a previously completed step to make changes or revisions, provide them with a link to do so. This can be accomplished in Flash by using ActionScript, which enables the developer to make Flash remember the steps a user has taken through a Flash movie.

Advantages of Designing Forms in Flash

We've discussed some of the common problems associated with forms designed in Flash; however, when used correctly, Flash-based forms can also offer some great benefits that improve the usability of the form. Flash designs offer a degree of fluidity that isn't often accomplished with HTML-based forms. It's important to keep things flowing smoothly for the users while they're in the process of entering information into a form. This helps keep them engaged and reduces the chance of distractions, which could break the users' concentration, causing them to abort the form process before they finish.

For instance, with Flash, a designer has the capability to make form posts (submitting form information and producing a result) without refreshing or reloading the page. This can be a great benefit to the users who can now see the result of their input immediately without having to wait for the form to submit or the page to refresh. Take, for example, the form used on Timbuk2's Bag Builder utility (Figure 5-14), which lets users create their own custom-designed bag. As a user proceeds through the form choosing various options, including bag style, colors, fabric, and accessories, their selections appear instantaneously in the bag diagram. When a user chooses an add-on accessory, an animated demonstration shows the accessory being added to the bag in the appropriate place. Even price changes are tracked and they show immediately on the selection of options that affect the price of the bag being "built." Don't like the color you picked? No problem—just click a different color and you'll see how it looks instantly. The use of Flash adds enormous value to this form. On-the-fly results mean users needn't wait for an entire page to submit and refresh before seeing the outcome of their selections. Animation helps users understand how a previously unfamiliar accessory looks and works on the bag. An overall engaging process keeps users interested throughout the bag-building process and helps them achieve their goal with a efficient, yet entertaining, approach.

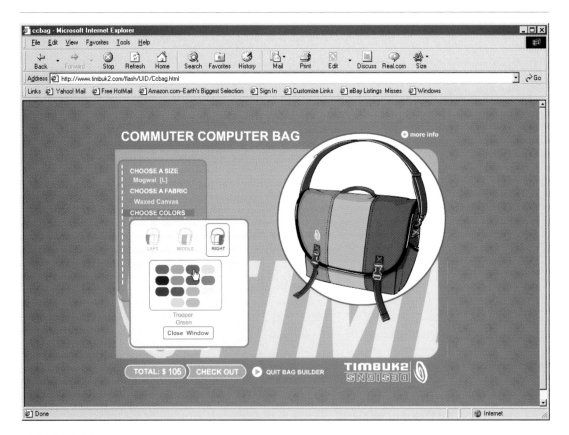

FIGURE 5-14

Timbuk2's Bag Builder Flash-based form provides users with a highly engaging and interactive shopping process

Knowing When Is Half the Battle

In some cases, Flash simply isn't the best option to use for your form. Depending on who your key users are and the overall purpose of the site you're designing, you might decide HTML is a more viable option for designing and developing your form. Remember—forms are an important means for gathering information from your users. If a user can't access a Flash form or isn't familiar enough with Flash to feel comfortable using it for a form process, you risk excluding a portion of your user base by not offering a non-Flash alternative. One option is to incorporate an HTML-based form within the Flash site. Another option is to offer users a non-Flash version of your entire site. (This option has other advantages as well when it comes to making your site accessible, which we'll discuss in Chapter 6.)

A word of caution if you go with the latter option, though. Make sure the users are in full control of which version of the site they're on. If you decide to offer two versions of the site—a Flash version and a non-Flash version—and a user chooses the Flash version, do not, as a result of a form action, take the user to the non-Flash version without their knowledge and consent. We've come across some sites that enable the user to access a form on the HTML version of the site from the Flash version. When the user submits the form from the Flash version, without warning they're taken to the HTML version of the site. Because the two versions typically have a somewhat different look or layout, this can be confusing to an unsuspecting user.

Summary

Great design without great content is like wrapping paper on an empty box—it lacks substance. The content is the meat of a site. Using our wrapped-box analogy, the navigation and labeling systems make up the structure or, in this case, the box. Design elements, like wrapping paper and bows, adorn the structure so it's appealing and interesting to the users. But the content inside the box must also be usable and appealing. Usability methods for great Flash design must be applied to all areas of the site, not only to the structure. Graphics, typography, animation, and forms are a few examples of elements that make up the content of a site. Regardless of how appealing the design is and how easily a user can get to the content, once there, they must continue to enjoy a positive experience. Otherwise, your efforts have been in vain.

Flash is a powerful design tool that, when used properly, can enhance both the graphic appeal and the usability of a site. In many cases, however, Flash-based content is a source of trouble for users because design often takes precedence over usability. In this chapter, we discussed some guidelines to overcome and avoid usability problems, and pointed out some ways in which Flash can be used to benefit the usability of web site content. By taking the time to incorporate these guidelines into your design, you can further ensure a positive experience throughout the users' stay on your site. In the next chapter, you get a closer look at the importance of making sure your site functions properly. We discuss user testing and accessibility as a means of ensuring the Flash content on your site works accordingly and is accessible to your target audience.

Flash Usability Fast Facts

) Four out of five web site users create bookmarks to relocate their favorite sites.

) Breaking up the content in a Flash movie into segments will allow users to individually bookmark sections within the movie.

) Avoid disabling the browser toolbar, which contains key navigational tools, including tools used to print and to bookmark content.

) Flash-based forms should be recognizable, learnable, and provide a means for the user to retrace their steps within the form-filling process.

) Flash-based forms offer the advantage of providing a smooth, fluid process for users because of the ability to make form posts without refreshing or reloading the page.

) When creating 2-D characters out of raster images, try breaking up the individual elements into different symbols so you can reduce bandwidth and increase your ability to animate the objects.

) Do not anti-alias pixel fonts, as it destroys the typography and makes text difficult to read.

) Use the Bandwidth Profiler to help create bandwidth-friendly Flash movies.

chapter

6

Making Sure It Works

In this chapter, you learn about web accessibility and user testing. *Accessibility* refers to how well a user can gain access to the content of your site. You look at some common accessibility problems that might prevent users from being able to access and interact with your site, focusing on those problems that most often affect Flash content. You also see some practical solutions to help ensure your content is accessible to all your target users.

Usability, as you already know, refers to how well users can interact with your site to accomplish their goals and how they perceive their overall experience on your site. To ensure your site is usable, testing with actual users should be conducted. An overview of general users' testing practices and processes is included near the end of this chapter. You learn why user testing is important and we present a systematic approach to conducting user testing on your own. The chapter concludes by looking at what to do with the results when you're done: evaluation and application.

Web Accessibility

The Internet is both the present and the future of modern communication. As the importance of the Internet increases, so do the number of people who need access to it. Users vary greatly in the types of equipment they use to access the Internet, and to complicate things a bit more, new technologies and devices—such as wireless and handheld computers, WebTV, and even cell phones—for accessing the Internet are entering the market at an increasing rate. Many of these devices are unable to display Flash content. As the number of people using alternate devices to access the Internet increases, so will the need for designers to accommodate these technologies through more accessible design and development methods. But hardware compatibility is not the only accessibility issue designers must address.

For people with physical disabilities, web accessibility is more than simply having hardware that's compatible with Flash content. Approximately 20 percent of the people in the United States have some type of disability, and for about half of those people, the disability can be considered severe. The majority of these people are limited in the ways in which they can use the Internet. For these people, even with the best equipment and Internet connection, accessing online content is difficult, if not impossible.

Although steps have been made toward increasing accessibility for people with disabilities, nearly 80 percent of the content currently on the Internet is at least partially inaccessible to them. The Web Accessibility Initiative (WAI) of the World Wide Web Consortium (W3C) was developed to provide technology, guidelines, tools, education, and research to promote accessibility for the disabled. Macromedia has included a section on its web site specifically devoted to accessibility and using Macromedia products to provide accessible web solutions. In October 2001, Macromedia went a step further by enlisting the services of the National Center for Accessible Media (NCAM) to assist in verifying the accessibility guidelines and information provided on its site. Macromedia's goal is to enable its customers (designers and developers using Macromedia products) to comply with Section 508 of the Rehabilitation Act by providing accessible solutions.

These initiatives are a step in the right direction, but ensuring that the Flash content being created meets the criteria outlined by these programs remains the responsibility of Flash designers and developers. Unfortunately, many designers and developers have not fulfilled this responsibility. To some, this might seem like a daunting task. Others might simply be unaware of the problem or feel it isn't a big enough problem to warrant spending the time and energy to fix. What many don't realize is this: by improving a site's accessibility for people with disabilities, the site's overall usability is often improved. For instance, when a site is made accessible for a deaf person, the site has also been made accessible to someone in an office environment who is accessing the Internet without a sound card installed in their computer.

The first step a designer must take is to develop an understanding of the problems people with disabilities face when trying to access Flash content on the Internet. To do that, let's look at some of the facts as they relate to people with disabilities. We'll focus on those disabilities that most commonly affect a person's ability to access Flash content—vision and hearing impairment.

Section 508: A Brief History

In 1998, Congress amended the Rehabilitation Act to include Section 508. The amendment was put in place to eliminate barriers in information technology, make new opportunities available for people with disabilities, and encourage the development of new technologies and products that would help realize this goal. Section 508 requires federal agencies to make their electronic and information technology accessible to people with disabilities. The law applies to all federal agencies when they develop, purchase, or use electronic and information technology, including web-based Internet and intranet systems. Under Section 508 (29 U.S.C. 794d), agencies must give employees and members of the public with disabilities access to information that's equivalent to the access provided to others. The Section 508 amendment also establishes a complaint process and reporting standards, thus further strengthening the law.

Section 508 does not apply to the private sector or to businesses using federal funds. Because of the magnitude of federal purchasing power, however, the belief is Section 508 will encourage competition in the technology industry. Federal agencies must purchase electronic and information technology that's accessible to disabled employees and the members of the public—because doing so doesn't place an undue burden on the agency. So, if two design-technology companies are bidding for a government contract and only one is offering a Section 508–compatible solution, that company is likely to win the business.

A complete list of the Section 508 standards can be found at http://www.section508.gov/final_text.html.

Visual Impairment

Approximately 10 million people in North America are visually impaired and at least 1.5 million visually impaired people use computers. Visual impairments range from *color blindness,* an inability to see or distinguish certain colors; to moderate visual impairments, which can be corrected with glasses or contact lenses; to uncorrectable low vision; to complete blindness. Because the Internet is primarily a visual experience, a limited ability or inability to use one's sense of sight presents unique challenges to both the individual affected by the disability and to the web designer who tries to make content accessible to these people.

Color Blindness

Color blindness is the least severe, but most common visual impairment. *Color blindness* is a genetic, sex-linked trait, which is much more prevalent in males than in females. About 10 percent of the male population and .5 percent of the female population experience some degree of color blindness. That's approximately one out of every ten male users on the Internet. Although color blindness is not considered a disability, it can affect a person's ability to view some content on the Web.

There are different degrees and types of color blindness. A person with true color blindness is completely unable to differentiate between certain problematic colors. This is the rarest form of color blindness. Most people with color blindness experience more of a color deficiency than a "blindness"; the majority are able to distinguish at least some difference between problematic colors, such as blue and yellow. About 99 percent of all color-blind people have trouble distinguishing between red and green, but can accurately detect black, white, and gray. In Figure 6-1, you can see what a red, yellow, green color scheme might look like to a color-blind user.

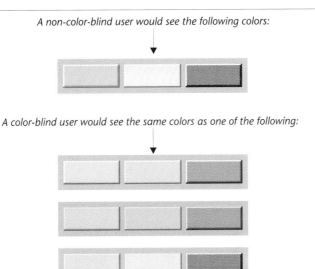

A non-color-blind user would see the following colors:

A color-blind user would see the same colors as one of the following:

FIGURE 6-1

This is a visual example of how the green, yellow, and red buttons might look to a person who is color-blind

Q & A From the Eyes of the Color-Blind: Interview with Chris Watts, Project Manager, ICON Multimedia

What aspects of sites that incorporate Flash content are difficult for you to use due to your color blindness?

All aspects of site interaction can be very difficult for a color-blind person if the colors used are within the spectrum affected by color blindness. For example, if the navigation elements for a site have green letters against a red background, they are invisible. Elements that use color change as a navigational or interactive aid become unusable; for example, the standard HTML hyperlink color is dark blue and the standard color for a link already visited is a lighter blue. These are often very difficult to view, especially against a similar-colored background.

What usability issues do you encounter on a daily basis while using your operating system?

I must set all background colors to white whenever possible, and I cannot use a desktop image with blue, purple, red, or green as a dominant color because text and other elements will blend into the background.

How do you overcome your color blindness when you are presented with color-coded navigation schemes?

Color-blind people use outlines to assist us when color becomes a problem. The first thing I do is try and determine the outline of what I am looking at. The next things I use are contextual clues. I look at the content of the next page to try and determine what the link was. I also use cursor changes to find links. Cursors that change from an arrow to a pointing hand are very useful.

If you could give advice to Flash developers to make their designs more accessible for color-blind users, what would it be?

When designing for people with color blindness, the same care, critical thinking, and detailed research that would be used to design for other disabilities is a must. Just as you would not use sound as a navigational cue for a deaf audience, certain color ranges should never be used as backgrounds, text colors, and especially not as navigational areas or areas of interactivity.

Guidelines for Designing for the Color-Blind   Because Flash content is most often designed in color, you should follow these guidelines to ensure that all users, including those who are color-blind, can use your site without any trouble or confusion.

) Avoid using color alone to convey important meanings or distinguish information, such as a site's navigation. Make sure noncolor cues, such as icons or text labels, are also available for people who are unable to see colors accurately.

) Avoid giving color-based instruction in your Flash content, such as "Select the green arrow to continue."

) Try to use bright colors whenever possible. Bright colors are easier to tell apart than dark (low value) or pastel colors.

) Avoid using problematic colors together (either next to or on top of one another). People who are red-green color-blind typically have difficulty distinguishing red, green, pink, orange, turquoise, aqua, and many shades of brown.

) Make strong contrasts between the background and the foreground in your Flash movies.

) Use ALT tags for images in case a color-blind user is unable to discern the image.

) Vischeck (http://www.vischeck.com) offers a free tool that checks the visibility of your graphics and text for color-blind users. The tool can show you what your content would look like to a person with various types of color blindness. You can upload an image file through its web site or download an Adobe Photoshop plug-in for Windows. You can also use the tool to check an entire web page by uploading a URL. This feature is currently in beta-testing, though, and won't work with Flash content.

) Colorfield (http://www.colorfield.com) offers a tool, called Colorfield Insight, for Mac users that models and predicts image legibility for color-deficient viewers. Colorfield currently supports Adobe Photoshop, Adobe Illustrator, Adobe After Effects, Adobe ImageReady, and Macromedia Fireworks applications. A free demo is available from its web site. Colorfield also offers an online simulation for three common types of color blindness.

Moderate Visual Impairment

About 9 million people (about 3.5 percent) in the United States alone have what's known as "low vision." The percentages are also similar in other parts of the world. People with low vision aren't completely blind, but their vision is limited to a degree that it affects the way in which they function; also, their vision cannot be corrected with typical prescription lenses. People with low vision require very large font sizes to read. When reading from a computer screen, low-vision users typically increase the font size (either on their own or with the help of a screen enlarger software program) to read the text. Flash content can be extremely difficult, and often impossible, for a low-vision person to view because of the tiny fonts often used and the inability (with most Flash content) to change the font size of text embedded in a Flash movie. Animated content can also pose problems because moving text is more difficult to read than static text. Flash does provide a powerful accessibility feature with Zoom In and Zoom Out controls. When this feature is enabled, users with visual impairments can magnify Flash graphics to more than 2000 percent of their original size with image quality (of vector graphics) maintained. Remember, if users choose to magnify text to a high degree, they might need to scroll both horizontally and vertically to be able to read it, and this functionality should also be provided.

Age-related visual impairments, such as glaucoma and cataracts, are also related to low vision. These conditions affect a person's ability to see clearly. People who have perfectly clear vision today might find themselves with a low-vision condition five or ten years from now. As the aging population grows, providing text and content that can be enlarged and limiting the amount of fast-moving animation will become increasingly important. The same people who are becoming familiar and comfortable with using the Internet today might be unable to do so in the future without these types of modifications.

Severe Visual Impairment

Nearly 200,000 people with *severe* visual impairments (little to no vision) have access to the Internet (United States Bureau of the Census, 1999). If your user base reaches outside the United States (as many do), the number of visually impaired people trying to access the Internet will be even higher. Unfortunately, most of them don't have access to many of the web sites on the Internet. The mouse and monitor are of little use to someone who is visually impaired. People with severe visual impairments typically access content on the Internet through the help of technology devices, such as Braille readers, which output content to a retractable Braille display that can then be read by touch, and screen readers that use synthesized speech software to "read" aloud the content displayed on the screen. Screen readers are unable to interpret the graphical content of images, and multimedia content such as Flash is completely uninterpretable unless an HTML version is available. For these devices to work properly, web content must be available in HTML format with ALT tags available for images. Also important is to make sure the content in the ALT tag is descriptive enough to provide an accurate "picture" for the user who is listening to it.

One of the biggest problems users of screen readers encounter is trying to understand how a web page is organized. A page that might be visually appealing and well organized to a sighted user might not make much sense to a user who must listen to the content of the page being read in a linear fashion. Pages that incorporate tables, graphs, or charts should be carefully analyzed to ensure they'll make logical sense when the data is read line-by-line.

Did You Know?

Macromedia offers a custom HTML template that helps developers export all the text and text equivalents of a Flash movie to HTML. This can then be interpreted by assistive devices, which are otherwise unable to understand Flash content. The template also makes providing equivalent content easier for users who don't have the Flash player installed. The template automatically generates code that detects whether users have the Flash player installed and provides an alternate image if they don't.

Hearing Impairment

The number of hearing-impaired individuals has steadily increased over the past few decades. More than 24 million people in the United States alone suffer from significant partial or complete loss of hearing. Approximately 40 percent of those are under the age of 65. The older a person becomes, the higher the incidence of hearing loss. By the age of 65, more than one-third of the population is affected by a significant hearing impairment.

Hearing impairments don't pose as many problems as visual impairments when trying to access web content. Most content on the Internet is either textual or visual, neither of which requires sound. Flash content, however, is a different story. Flash movies and animations usually include, and sometimes require, the use of sound to be fully effective. Music is often used along with visual cues to convey a certain style or image. Sound is sometimes used in the form of voice-overs that provide instructions to a user on how to use the Flash content. When Flash is used to create entertainment-based content, sound is almost always a part of the experience. Flash-based games typically incorporate an extensive use of sound, sometimes as a background effect, but often as a cue to let the user know what's going on in the game. The use of sound typically becomes a problem for hearing-impaired users only when the content being viewed relies on or requires sound to be understood and used effectively.

One way to ensure the use of sound isn't a problem is to provide users with the capability to turn the sound on or off. Doing so can offer a number of benefits. First, users who are able to hear, but who don't want to listen to the sound, can turn it off. Second, by designing with the idea in mind that the user might choose to turn off the sound, you'll be less likely to incorporate elements that require sound to function properly. Another approach is to provide synchronized captions and/or transcripts for the audio portion of the content. This is particularly helpful if you're designing a Flash piece that requires sound to be understood. Remember, users will be reading this content instead of listening to it, which might require that you slow the movie down a bit or enable the user to stop, pause, and rewind the content on their own.

Did You Know?

Macromedia Flash gives developers the capability to provide user controls to stop, pause, fast forward, or rewind Macromedia Flash content. Doing so enables users to replay the content as needed.

Technology-Based Impairments

Even if a user has no physical impairments, their experience on the Internet might still be affected because of technology deficiencies or limitations.

Users who have older computers with slow processors, 56K connections, and small, low-resolution, low-color depth screen displays might feel impaired when trying to view Flash content. Some users are hindered because of the environment in which they're accessing the Internet. For example, a user in an office environment might not have a sound card installed or enabled and, therefore, is unable to hear audio files that accompany Flash content.

Following design guidelines that ensure accessibility for users with physical disabilities often solves many of the problems faced by users with technology-based impairments and typically results in a better overall site experience for all users.

Web Accessibility Resources for Flash

A number of additional resources are available to assist designers and developers in the creation of accessible content. Perhaps the most well known is the W3C WAI. *WAI* is a program whose mission is to promote a high degree of usability on the Web for people with disabilities. WAI offers guidelines, tips, techniques, checklists, and evaluation tools to assist designers and developers in creating accessible content. The WAI resources can be found at http://www.w3.org/WAI/Resources/.

Macromedia offers accessibility resources specifically devoted to Flash design and development. It has partnered with NCAM to deliver improved accessibility options with Flash, which enables its designers and developers to comply with Section 508. Macromedia's site offers design techniques and developer resources to help improve the accessibility of Flash content. Macromedia's Flash Accessibility Resource Center can be found at http://www.macromedia.com/software/flash/productinfo/accessibility/.

Did You Know?

According to Macromedia, an upcoming version of the Flash player will enable access to underlying data within a Flash (SWF) file, permitting the text within to be interpreted by assistive devices, such as screen readers. Developers will be able to expose their Flash content, making properties (such as scale and visibility) adjustable and controllable by end users.

User Testing

Unfortunately, no scientific formula exists for designing and developing a completely usable web site. Designers can be aware of general usability guidelines and know how to apply them to Flash content, but that's no guarantee of usability. A Flash developer's most *valuable* resource for ensuring usability is feedback from actual users.

The purpose of user testing is to discover problems a user might encounter when trying to access, view, or interact with your site. Users will find and point out problems you never dreamed existed. They'll provide you with feedback on what they like and what they don't like, and perhaps even offer an opinion or two on how they think your site could be improved.

User testing isn't a focus group or a survey—it's a one-on-one observance of an actual user interacting with an actual site. By assessing how successful users are at completing their goals while using your site and how satisfied they are with their experience as a whole, you'll be able to validate whether your site achieves its objective for your target audience.

Why User Testing Is Important

Let's assume you've done your homework before diving into the design and development of a site. You took the time to sort out the purpose of your site, the goals of your users, and what they need and don't need. You even developed a few user profiles to keep your target at the forefront of your mind as you planned the site. So why bother with user testing? After all, wasn't the time you spent up front getting to know what your users want and need supposed to reduce the chances of designing or developing an unusable site?

Reduce the chances—yes. Eliminate the chances—no. How an actual user will act and react to an interactive experience is difficult to predict. The research and experience of others is helpful in learning about what *generally* works and what doesn't. It can help you avoid making the mistakes others have already learned from the hard way. But there's no substitute from real-world feedback from your real-world users.

The problem of your own personal bias and overfamiliarity with the site is another reason to test. You've eaten, slept, and breathed the site for longer than you'd like to recall. You know it inside and out, and rightly so—you designed and built it. At this point, you've probably begun developing a relationship with the site—a personal connection to what you created. To honestly and accurately critique something that reflects your own personal opinion, talent, and expertise is difficult. In addition, what seems simple, logical, and self-explanatory to you might not seem so to a user who's never seen or interacted with your site before. It's important to get a fresh set of nonbiased eyes to provide some honest feedback on both the good and the bad of your site.

User testing has financial benefits as well. The time required for user testing your site early on will be small in comparison to the time required to redesign and/or redevelop a site that you later find is unusable. Unfortunately, user testing is often put on the back burner because clients and developers alike are under the impression that it requires large amounts of time, money, and resources to test a site adequately. In fact, just the opposite is true. User testing can be done in a short amount of time (as little as a day), on a small budget, with minimal resources. And the benefits will far outweigh the costs. Usability problems cost companies hundreds of thousands of dollars. Many of these problems could have easily been detected during the development stage with some simple user testing. According to Forrester Research, companies forfeit approximately 50 percent of online sales because people can't find items on the site and 40 percent of users who have a negative experience on their first visit to a site never return. Those are staggering figures! When you consider that a majority of the usability problems a site experiences could have been eliminated if user testing had been done during development, the decision about whether to test should be an easy one. In the end everyone—you, your clients, and your users—will benefit.

What to Test and When to Test

Testing and evaluation should be an iterative, ongoing process. Ideally, you should test your site at various points throughout the design and development.

User testing is especially important with Flash-based content because of the variety of components Flash incorporates. Animation, color, sound, and text all play an important role in the makeup of a Flash movie. And, with each new component comes a new opportunity for a usability glitch to appear. Predicting how users will react to something they've never (or have only seldom) encountered on the Web is difficult. Testing your Flash designs on real live users is a sure-fire way to determine whether you're on the right track or need to return to the drawing board.

Table 6-1 presents a handy overview of each testing phase described in the following sections.

Project Phase	What to Test	What to Test For	How to Incorporate the Results
Preplanning	A current or previous version of the site you'll be working on	What the site does well and where it fails.	Benchmark against best practices.
			Avoid/correct problems.
	A competitor's web site		
Design concept	Paper interface mock-ups or wireframes	Do users understand the initial design, organization, and labeling?	If the feedback is positive and you find you're on the right track, stay on it and move forward.
	Nonfunctional web-based screen mock-ups	Does the content seem of value? Will it meet users' needs?	If the feedback is negative and you find you've missed the mark, use comments and feedback to fix the problems.
	Storyboards for Flash movie		
	Site map showing content organization and labeling		
Prototype	Working prototype of site (partial or full site)	Are users able to interact effectively with the site?	Add instruction or functionality where necessary to help users better understand how to interact with the site.
	Working Flash content	Do users understand how to accomplish key tasks?	
		Is anything on the site confusing or unclear?	Modify or eliminate elements that cause confusion to users.
		Is anything about the site keeping users from being able to accomplish their goals?	Modify or eliminate elements that keep users from accomplishing their goals.
Prelaunch	Final working site, including all Flash elements	Retest for the same things you did at the prototype stage.	Make final modifications based on user feedback before the site goes live.
		Make sure you adequately addressed the problems found in the prototype stage.	Make sure all usability issues have been effectively addressed.

TABLE 6-1

Overview of Phase-by-Phase Iterative Testing

Preplanning Phase Testing

Preplanning is the phase of a project when you're gathering information and planning how you'll accomplish meeting the business and user goals for the site. This is a good time to test to get an idea of the direction you should head with your site design. Because you probably won't have done any designs of your own yet, try testing with some sites that are already available.

If your project involves redesigning an existing web site, conduct your user testing on the current or previous version of the site. If your project involves designing a site from scratch, see if you can find a few competitors' sites to test. The feedback you get can provide you with valuable information as to what users like and what they don't like, what works and what doesn't work. You can use this information to avoid making mistakes that have already been made. You can also use it to incorporate *best practices*—things you already know work well—into your site design.

Design Concept Phase Testing

In this phase, you want to start testing for your user's reactions to your concept designs. You might not have a web-based interface to test with at this point, but that's okay. Even if you don't have a web-based interface, you can conduct your test using some paper screen mock-ups or even a site map. In both cases, you can show your users the direction you're heading with the organization, labeling, and information flow of the site. If you're developing Flash content, you can test that here, too, using storyboards to show the users how the movie will flow, and what they'll see and be able to do in each frame. You're testing here for the users' initial reaction to the site—do they understand it? Does the organization and labeling you've chosen seem logical to them? Is anything missing? Ask them if they think the site is one they'd visit in the future, along with some feedback as to why or why not. Ask them for their opinions on how you could improve the content or design. An outside user might come up with an idea or solution to improve the site plan that you hadn't considered. At this stage in the project, it's easy (and inexpensive) to make changes. And, small changes made now can help you avoid bigger usability problems down the road.

Prototype Testing

Once you reach the *prototype* stage of a project, you should have some working site models and Flash content available for testing. You might even have a complete prototype site at this point. Your testing at this stage will be similar to the testing you did on the live sites in the preplanning stage. You're trying to find out what works well and what doesn't. Ideally you will have incorporated any necessary changes that resulted from your previous phase of testing. Now you can see how those changes have affected your users' ability to accomplish their goals. This will be your first chance to see how a user actually interacts with your site. Can users get where they need to go and do what they need to do? Do they like the way the site looks? How about the Flash content—do your users understand it? Do they like the content or is there something they find annoying that can easily be fixed?

This is the time to find out, so you can make any final changes before the site goes live.

Prelaunch Testing

This is it—your last chance to make sure your users can (and will) use your site. You should have a fully functioning, ready-to-go-live site to test with now. If you tested the site iteratively, you shouldn't find any major, new usability problems now. At this stage, you're testing to double-check and fine-tune everything on the site. Retest any elements or tasks that caused problems in previous tests to make sure you corrected the problem. Try some free-form testing as well—give your testers a chance to surf freely through the content on your site. Listen to them, watch their reactions, and try to find out how closely what you've presented them matches their expectations. You still have time to tweak the site if necessary.

Who to Test

When choosing your test subjects, you want to find users who are representative of your target audience. In Chapter 3, you learned about profiling your target users. Taking the time to do this early on not only helps you design and develop with an idea in mind of who you're designing for, it also gives you a clear picture of the types of people you need to find to test your site. Don't test the site on your mom if her profile doesn't match that of your target users. If you're having a hard time gaining access to representative users because of geographical boundaries or other constraints, try to come as close as possible to test users with similar characteristics. In this case, the key characteristics you should try to match most closely include

> Similar Internet experience and familiarity (including familiarity with plug-ins such as Flash)

> Similar level of education

> Similar occupation (if their occupation would affect their use of and expectations for the site)

> Similar nationality/primary language

> Similar familiarity with the type of content presented on your site. For example, if you're designing a site targeted mainly at automotive

engineering professionals, finding test subjects with an understanding of the automotive engineering industry is important.

Try to get a minimum of five test subjects. According to many usability experts, 80 percent of the usability problems in a site can be uncovered with as few as five testers. Try to make sure each of your target user groups is represented among your test subjects. If you determined earlier that you have one primary user group and three secondary user groups, try to find two representatives from your primary audience and one from each of your three secondary audiences. Because different user groups have different needs, goals, and characteristics, it's important to get feedback from each group.

What You'll Need

A common excuse for not testing a web site is the lack of an appropriate usability lab in which to conduct the test. This is no longer a valid excuse. Why? Because you don't need a fancy usability lab to conduct user testing. In fact, you don't need a lab at all. Here's what you do need:

) A quiet location (an office or a conference room is usually a good choice)

) A couple of chairs (one for the test subject, one for each observer)

) A desk or table

) Paper and pen/pencil

) A computer (if you're testing an actual interface)

) An Internet connection (if you're testing a live site)

) Video camera (not a necessity, but helpful)

Try to make sure the computer equipment and Internet connection you're testing with is representative of the equipment and connection your actual users will use to access your site. If the majority of your users will access your site using a middle-of-the-road PC and connecting to the Internet through a 56K modem, then testing your site with the latest high-tech equipment and broadband connection won't give you an accurate assessment of how the site will function for your user. The Flash content you developed might download quickly and work fine on your own equipment, but the test you conduct should tell you whether it will function equally well in your users' environment.

Executing the Test

Now that you know what to test, when to test, who to test, and where to test, you need to know how to test. Remember, you're trying to find out how real users will interact with your site. You need to get their feedback and reaction to what you've designed and developed. How you carry out the test depends somewhat on the phase of the project you're in and what you're testing. In general, though, you want to set up your test in a quiet room where distractions will be minimal. If you have a video camera, set it in the corner, pointed toward your user—try to make the camera as inconspicuous as possible because some testers might get stage fright if they know they're being taped.

Test only one test subject at a time, so you're able to devote your full attention to them. Provide clear instructions up front as to what you'd like them to do. Make it clear to your tester that there are no wrong answers and it's not possible to fail the test. Some testers can get distracted trying to impress you with the "right" answers and lose the ability to focus on using the site as they would in real life. During the test, try not to offer any help to your tester (other than the initial instructions). If your tester gets stuck, let them figure out how to get unstuck. Part of what you're trying to learn is how someone would interact with the site in real life, and getting unstuck is part of real-life interaction. This can also provide you with valuable information on how you can improve the design of the site.

Live-Site Testing

Live-site testing usually takes place in the preplanning and prelaunch stages of a project. You're testing on a site that's live or functioning as though it were live—usually a current version of the site you're redesigning, a competitor's site, or a prototype of your site shortly before it's finished.

Take some time to put together a list of goals you want your test subjects to accomplish on your test sites. The goals you come up with should match the goals you think an actual user might have on the site. For instance, if you're testing in the preplanning stage and are using a competitor's interactive Flash module on how to operate its cellular phone, come up with several tasks a user might want to accomplish on the site. You might ask the test subject to find out how to access their voice mail system. Or, you might give them the task of figuring out how their stored phone list works and ask them how they would add and/or delete a phone number from it. The key is to come up with tasks you think an actual user might want to accomplish on the site. You're looking for the elements and characteristics of the site that help the user accomplish the goal and the elements that cause problems.

You can also test for other non-task-related things on a live site. Try asking your testers some open-ended questions about their perception of the site, such as how the site looks to them. Is your site visually appealing? Can they understand just by looking at it what the purpose of the site is and what it will enable them to do? Remember, to a user, perception is often reality and this plays a big part in how a user feels about their overall experience. Have paper and pencil handy to jot down notes and observations during each test. This is especially important if you don't have the luxury of a video camera to tape the test.

Concept Testing

During the design concept phase of a project, you probably won't have a fully functional version of the site to test. That's okay—you can still gather some valuable information at this stage by conducting a few simple user tests. Show your tester a concept design (either on paper or on a screen) that depicts the organization, navigation, and labeling scheme you plan to use. Ask the tester to navigate out loud through each section and tell you what they think they'll find or be able to do. If you developed an initial look and feel for your site, also show that to the tester to find out if it's visually appealing to them, and if it invokes the right feelings and emotional responses to the site.

You can also conduct concept testing on your Flash movies using storyboards. Show the tester the flow of the movie in storyboard format and note where they'll be able to interact with the movie (if interaction will be possible). Your tester can provide you with feedback on a number of different issues. Does the Flash movie make sense to them in the context of the rest of the site? Does it fit well within the site? Does the Flash movie seem too long or too short? Does it offer any value to them—is it something they'd take the time to watch and interact with? The answers to these questions can tell if you used Flash to provide value and enhance the experience or if you used Flash only for the sake of using Flash. If you find the answer is the latter, you should rethink your design strategy.

Evaluating and Applying the Results

When you're through with a particular round of testing, compile your results so you can review and evaluate them. Divide the results of your feedback into two lists—things that were good about the site and things that caused problems or need improvement. Review each list and note the amount of feedback received on each item. If all five of your testers commented on how easy it was to find what they needed on the site you tested, then your navigation scheme is probably pretty good. If four out of five users couldn't figure out how to turn off the sound in the Flash movie on your site, then it's probably something that needs to be addressed. If the positive feedback you received was during the preplanning phase on a competitor's site, keep it in mind and try to incorporate similar elements in your own site. We're not saying to copy your competitor's web site, but if something works well, don't reinvent the wheel. If you received negative feedback on a competitor's site, remember that as an opportunity to develop a competitive advantage by overcoming the problem on your own site.

Next, take a second look at your list of problems and review each one—not in terms of how much feedback you received, but in terms of the effect each problem will have on your site. According to Jakob Nielsen, three categories of usability problems exist.

> **Catastrophes**   Problems that prevent a user from completing a goal

> **Serious Usability**   Problems that slow down a user significantly, but don't completely prevent the completion of a goal

> **Cosmetic**   Problems that annoy users or slow them down slightly, but don't have a serious effect on how well they can accomplish their goals

About half of the problems you find during testing will most often fall into the third category—cosmetic problems. Cosmetic problems won't typically stop users from using your site, but they might annoy users so much they don't want to use it. These are things like being unable to turn off the sound on a Flash movie. The good thing about cosmetic problems is this: although they might account for the majority of your usability issues, they typically are relatively easy to fix.

About a third of the problems detected during testing will fall into the more severe category—serious usability problems. An example of this would be a Flash movie that takes forever to download on a user's computer. Having to wait a long time for a movie to download would certainly slow down the user's ability to accomplish their goal on your site. Being unable to find the navigation on the site because it's been hidden is another example of a serious usability problem. Serious usability problems vary in the amount of time and effort they take to correct. The good news is catching a problem like this early on will be much easier to fix than if you wait until the site has already gone live. This is one of the key reasons to do iterative testing throughout the development process.

You may or may not find problems that fall into the third category—catastrophes. Catastrophes are problems that thwart a user's efforts to accomplish their goal. An example of a catastrophe is a site you designed entirely in Flash without offering an alternative (HTML) version. A user who is unable to use Flash to view the site won't be able to access it. This might not seem like a big problem, but the inability to print the contents of a Flash-based presentation might also be considered a catastrophe-type usability problem if this was a goal the user hoped to accomplish on the site. How you rate a particular problem might vary from site to site because the seriousness is determined greatly by the goals of the user. For instance, the previous example used of being unable to print Flash content might not be a catastrophe at all if printing isn't a goal any of your users have. This is another reason why it's important to know and understand your user's goals.

Summary

As the importance of the Internet continues to grow, so too will the importance of making sure the content you design and develop is both accessible and usable. The Internet holds great potential for increasing the independence and enriching the lives of people who suffer from disabilities. To do so, though, the Internet must be accessible to them. Those responsible for designing and developing sites must take the time to ensure the final product is accessible to all the users in their target audience. User testing is one way to check the accessibility and usability of your design. By subjecting your design to the inspection and judgment of actual users, you can gain valuable feedback that can be used to improve the overall experience had by the people who use your site. This is a step you simply can't afford to skip. In an industry that's demanding more and tolerating less, designing sites that are both accessible and usable is no longer *optional*.

Flash Fast Facts

❭ Make sure to include ALT tags for images and animations. If you're designing a site entirely in Flash, provide an HTML version, which can be interpreted by a screen-reading device, for those who are unable to view the Flash site.

❭ Provide visually impaired users with a way to enlarge the text within a Flash movie, either by embedding HTML text within the movie or enabling the zoom feature.

❭ Avoid designing elements that require the use of sound to be understood and used effectively. In cases where sound is necessary to understand the content, provide synchronized textual captions, so users who are unable to hear the sound can still understand the content.

❭ User testing and evaluation should be an iterative process done throughout the design and development of the site.

❭ Testing can be done early in the development process using paper screen mock-ups and storyboards for Flash movies.

❭ You can typically uncover about 80 percent of a site's usability problems with five test subjects.

❭ Make sure the test subjects you recruit are representative of your actual target user groups.

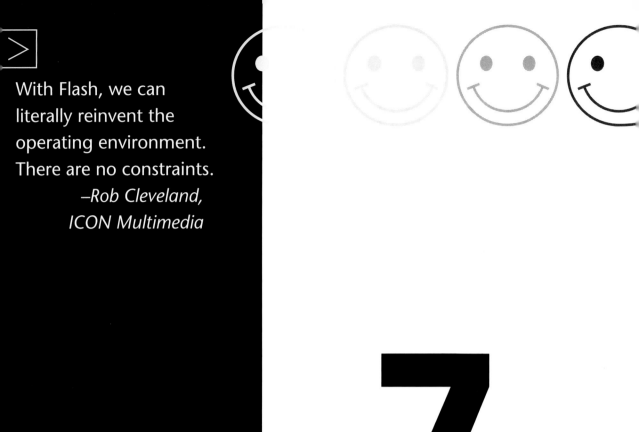

> With Flash, we can
> literally reinvent the
> operating environment.
> There are no constraints.
> –Rob Cleveland,
> ICON Multimedia

chapter  **7**

Case Study: ICON Multimedia's Web Site

In this chapter, we present a case study on a Flash site redesign. The goal of this chapter is to illustrate how Flash designers can maintain good design and usability at the same time. This chapter starts with a general critique of the site from information architect Louis Rosenfeld. Using before and after screens, we illustrate how to make the site more usable, while maintaining the original vision for the design.

Background

This chapter focuses on a site coauthor Kevin Airgid designed two years ago for ICON Multimedia. The original objective of the site was to showcase the company services and information in a unique and highly creative Flash interface. The Flash site was built completely by the designer. At this time, the company didn't have the benefit of an information architect. Many Flash developers have similar situations when they're developing Flash content. The site critique and fix to follow help illustrate real-world solutions to common usability problems Flash developers encounter every day.

The Site Critique

We wanted to get a professional, nonbiased opinion of the site, so we asked well-known information architect Louis Rosenfeld to look at it and provide us with some feedback. We asked Lou to pay specific attention to the use of Flash throughout the site and to give feedback on such things as what frustrated him, what annoyed him, and what contributed to the overall experience, making it either positive or negative. We knew going into this review that the response and feedback weren't going to be pretty.

Lou's Experience with www.iconideas.com

Lou Rosenfeld is an independent information architecture consultant based in Ann Arbor, Michigan. He was cofounder and president of Argus Associates, long recognized as an industry leader in information architecture consulting. Lou also coauthored *Information Architecture for the World Wide Web* (O'Reilly, 1998) with Peter Moville, which Amazon.com lauded as the "Best Internet Book of 1998." Lou has been a regular contributor for *Internet World, CIO,* and *Web Review* magazines, and he consults for such Fortune 500 clients as Ford Motor Company and Hewlett-Packard.

Here is Lou's account:

At the authors' request, I had a look at the ICON Multimedia web site (http://www.iconideas.com). "It's full of Flash," they said. "Let us know what you think."

Umm. OK, I've been forewarned. And, although I like to complain about almost everything under the sun, I should go a little easy here. After all, Kevin *did* design it.

But this site is a perfect example of why so many people absolutely despise Flash-based sites. This is too bad, as Flash is just a tool like any other, extremely useful in some cases, and not at all in others. But here, the designer succumbed to an exciting new technology as if it were the newest designer drug and is willing to drag all the site's users along on what turns out to be a bad trip.

Here's how my trip unfolds.

I load http://www.iconideas.com. Front and center, on the main page, I am (again) forewarned by a notice: What We Do: Flash... OK, so I imagine I'll encounter some Flash along the way. Good enough.

So I click Enter and ... ARGHHH!

The whole browser is taken over by Flash! Or is it? I desperately want to back up to see if there is a non-Flash version of the site available, but I can't. Instead, now I have two windows to worry about: the original browser window, which affords me important, useful, and conventional navigational comforts, such as telling me where I am, and this new one that removes the URL field from the browser window.

Why exactly is it that I need two windows to view one site?

So, now I'm stuck in the Flash window. I notice an arrow labeled Navbar. I guess that it points me to where I should click to reach the navigation bar. On most other sites, I wouldn't need to have this pointed out to me; it would be there, awaiting my click. Instead, this one is hidden away, and I have to mess with a tab to get it to show.

Grumpily, I mess with it. In turn, it messes with me: it makes noises, undulates, throbs, and changes the appearance of the whole window. In fact, the bar itself is no bar, but a vertical field that takes over half the browser window, obscuring what might be valuable context on the page I started from. Just what exactly is the value this provides to users?

I decide to have a look at the Careers area. I notice all the copy is bitmapped, which means I can't copy-and-paste it into an e-mail to forward along to a friend. And, because this is a Flash window, there is nothing for me to bookmark for my friend. That's too bad for my friend and too bad for the ICON folks as well. Must all text be rendered in image format? I'm guessing the only reason is that fixed image sizes enable the designer to control window dimensions, allowing for proper display by ... Flash!

Grumble.

I click on Contact Us, and the address and other contact information slide up from the bottom of the screen. Fine, but this doesn't work like the rest of the navigation system. A strike against consistency. Is Flash at fault here? I don't know. But I have my suspicions.

Next I click on Main Screen. Hmmm ... I see from the press release blurbs that ICON has hired an information architect. I'd like to learn more.

Click.

Up pops a new window. Seems to have some sort of scrolling apparatus on the right-hand edge of the window, which takes me four or five clicks to learn how to use.

By now, hundreds of millions of dollars have been invested into designing GUI operating systems, not to mention web browsers. But here, thanks to Flash, the designer gets to reinvent the wheel, with his own take on how scrolling should work. His take loses me, at least temporarily. I'm not against experimentation, but I'm not sure this is the place to reinvent the user interface.

And, by the way, I'm now ready to give up, which I do. Listen, I'm not really as bad as I sound. Some of my best friends are designers. And new technologies, like Flash, are exciting. They make it easy to design new things and push the envelope further.

But they also make it possible to make new mistakes. When a designer first gets his hands on a hammer (like Flash), every problem looks like a nail. More mistakes get made. More users get frustrated. And we all end up going back to the drawing board. This is part of the natural evolution of web design, but I hope and pray this book helps readers to learn from others' mistakes, instead of making them over and over again.

–Louis Rosenfeld
http://www.louisrosenfeld.com
lou@louisrosenfeld.com

The Problems

Well, there you have it. Just as we suspected, Lou's experience was everything but pleasant. Unfortunately, and also as we suspected, much of the trouble he encountered was directly related to the way Flash was used to design and develop the site.

Let's sum up some of the problems Lou pointed out (and add a few we noticed as well):

) The site is offered in Flash only, leaving users who are unable to view Flash content without access to the information contained on the site.

) The site requires two windows—one for the splash page and one that contains the actual site. This seems unnecessary and potentially confusing.

) The window that displays the content of the site overtakes the user's entire screen, leaving them without important navigational tools such as the URL display.

) The navigation is hidden and difficult to use. As Lou commented, why not make it readily available to the users instead of making them do extra work to get to it? As a general rule, given the choice, it's always best to avoid hiding the navigation.

) The label Navbar might not be easily and immediately understood by all users. Labels should be self-explanatory, familiar, and easy to interpret. Abbreviations should generally be avoided. Why the designer chose Main Screen instead of Home as the label for the link to the home page also seems unclear. Home is a more familiar term to users.

❭ The vertically sliding tab-button navigation system is difficult to use even after you learn how it works. For instance, when a user clicks a subnavigation category tab (such as Design Gallery), it slides vertically partway across the screen. Now the user has an even smaller vertical window to read text in and it's partially covering the page it slid over. Closing the vertical field can be done by reclicking the tab, but this is only realized through a trial-and-error-based process.

❭ Each time users navigate to a new section, they have to wait for the content to load, which can be both annoying and a waste of time.

❭ The nonstandard scroll bars are difficult to use. Creativity doesn't mean reinventing the operating system.

❭ The font size seems small and the color (light gray) is difficult to read against a white background. A larger font and better contrast between the background color and font color would make the site easier to view, as well as more accessible to people with vision deficiencies.

❭ When a user tries to print the content, it prints exactly as shown on the screen (in vertical format), which wastes paper. Because the text on most of the pages throughout the site is unselectable, the user is also unable to copy-and-paste it into, perhaps, a Word document, which would be easier and more efficient to print.

❭ The "bounciness" effect that occurs whenever a tab is opened is distracting and doesn't seem to add any value to the site.

❭ The sound associated with the navigation is disruptive and can't be turned off from the site. Again, it adds little value to the experience.

❭ Some basic functionality seems to be missing from the site that would enhance the experience for users. For example, when a user clicks Contact, the address, phone, and e-mail information located at the bottom of the page is simply shifted to the top. The user would then have to call, write, or go into their e-mail program and send an e-mail to contact the company. Why not make it easier on the user with an online contact form that could easily be filled out and submitted directly from the site?

❯ The content in the Careers section also seems to be missing some basic functional features. Lou mentioned possibly wanting to tell a friend about a job he saw posted on ICON's site. Providing the functionality for him to do this with the click of a button would be a nice addition to the site. And what about someone who wants to submit their resume to ICON? Instead of simply providing an e-mail address on the site, why not include an online form a user could fill out and use to attach his resume?

Overall, it seems like Flash was used only for the sake of using Flash. Flash wasn't used to add any value to the site or to the overall experience. In addition, it seems some basic and useful features and functionality were neglected, perhaps because the focus was on how to make the site "cool" and unique, rather than on how to meet the needs and goals of the users who might be visiting the site.

The Site Fix

The following is commentary by Kevin Airgid, the Flash designer of the http://www.iconideas.com site. Kevin explains the rationale behind the Flash site and demonstrates effective ways to solve the usability issues while maintaining the spirit of the original design. In most circumstances, retooling a Flash site to meet usability standards is not the preferred method. The best practice would be to redesign the site completely from the ground up with usability as your guide. For illustration purposes, we show before and after shots of the same site design. In doing this, we help to illustrate how parts of the graphic user interface could have been designed to make this site more usable.

Here are Kevin's comments:

Lou hit the mark when he commented "the designer succumbed to an exciting new technology as if it were the newest designer drug and is willing to drag all the site's users along on what turns out to be a bad trip." When I built this site, I was trying to showcase how creative I could be with Flash. By designing a nonstandard interface element, I hoped to show the potential of the type of creative work we could produce as a company. I think many other Flash developers fall into this trap. They design unique and creative Flash sites but, in the end, these sites are hard to use. I do believe that as designers, we need to find the middle ground between form and function. I did not intend to take my users on a "bad trip," as Lou describes it. My intention was to show users how creative a Flash site could be. What I didn't realize at the time was that creativity should never come at the expense of usability.

Creativity and usability can enhance each other. Now, in retrospect, almost a year and half after building this site, I've learned many things about usability. I think my most important discovery is that Flash can be unique and creative without running over the user. By this, I mean Flash designers don't need to create new interface elements or take over the user's screen to make a Flash site an extraordinary experience. An extraordinary Flash experience comes as a result of well-designed, well-organized content that uses Flash to enhance the experience with engaging, entertaining, and easy-to-use elements.

The first step to improve this site would be enhancing the splash screen (see Figure 7-1). This splash screen would serve as a place where users could choose if they wanted to view the Flash site or the HTML site. This would enable users to skip to an HTML version if they didn't want to view Flash even if they had the plug-in installed. Just because users have the Flash plug-in doesn't necessarily mean they want to view Flash animation. The new version of this site has a custom content-management system populating the content, so maintaining content between the two sites is easy because it comes from the same database.

One of the reasons I chose to make the main screen take over the whole screen was because I wanted the design to employ large areas of white space for a clean look. I also wanted to make the single image on the screen large. In doing this, I needed a large area to display it in, so I took over the screen. This made the site minimal in design, but it did nothing for usability. This removed many of the browser interface elements users are comfortable with. In the redesigned version, I maintained the minimal look by reducing the size of the image to fit visually into a 800×600 browser window. By returning the browser back to normal, I gave back to users their ability to bookmark pages using the browser menus (now Lou can e-mail the URL to his friend!). By displaying the normal browser window, the users could also see the URL change as they moved from page to page.

To address the problem of type readability, I set the font to not anti-alias and I bumped up the font size to 13 points. The paragraph width was also

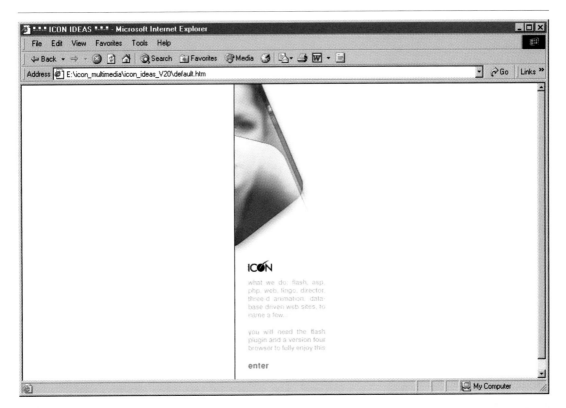

FIGURE 7-1

Site splash screen

increased to reduce the amount of scrolling a user would do to read the text. I also made this text area selectable, so users could copy the text if they wanted. To address the problem of printing the text, I used the Macromedia Printing SDK and created a Print button, so users could print the information on each page. I removed the site's tabs that made the large vertical areas slide open. Although this was a cool effect, it did not enhance the site's message and it did not add value. Users who want to see cool animation can look in the Portfolio section of the site to see useful examples of animation.

The animated/hidden navigation was a nuisance to many users because it increased the time it took to go from one section to another, making the site tedious to use after only a few clicks. Now that the gray tabs are removed (see Figures 7-2 and 7-3), the design becomes cleaner looking

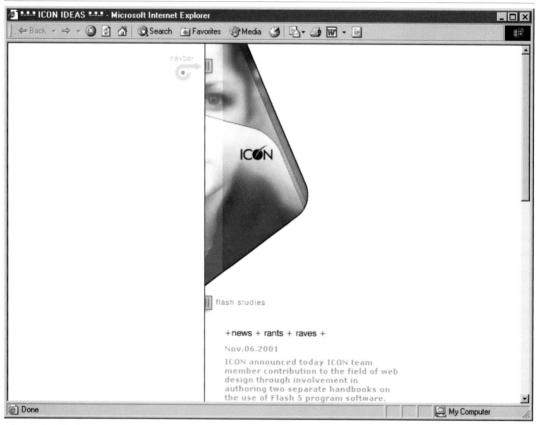

FIGURE 7-2

Flash site home page before redesign

because the vertical line isn't dotted by heavy gray buttons breaking its vertical descent down the page. A slight restructuring of the design brought increased usability, without destroying the clean look of the site. Also, I removed the sound from the rollovers on the navigation bar because they didn't add any value (see Figure 7-4).

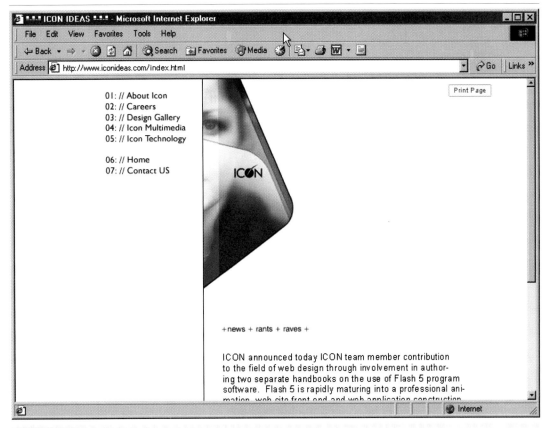

FIGURE 7-3

Flash site after redesign

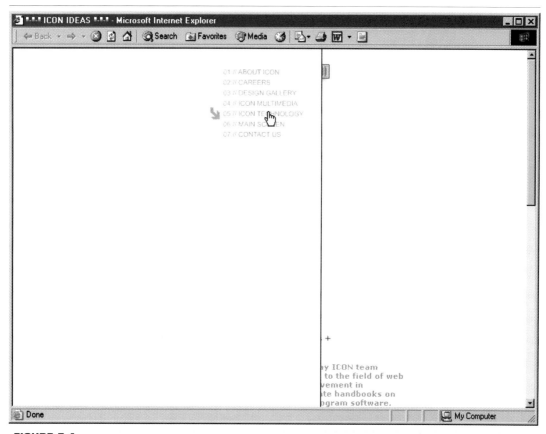

FIGURE 7-4

Original hidden Flash navigation with sound and blinking arrow rollover

To solve the problem with the nonstandard scrollbar on the press release area, I created more standard-looking interface elements, as shown in Figure 7-5. These elements look better in the design because the user's attention is drawn to the content, rather than to the interface elements used to scroll the content. I think many Flash developers venture down this path—they lose sight of the content and spend too much time on the interface: the content should always be your first consideration. A good interface is one the user doesn't notice and the Flash interface should enhance the content, not distract from it.

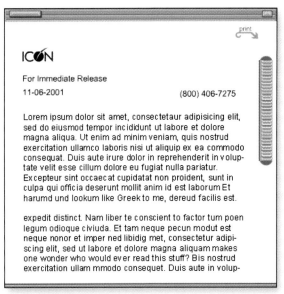

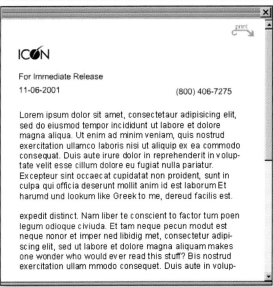

FIGURE 7-5

Nonstandard scroll interface for press releases (top); redesigned scroll interface (bottom)

In the Careers section, shown in Figure 7-6, we redesigned it with two new options (see Figure 7-7). Users can recommend a job to a friend or upload their resumes through the Apply For Job button. This can help make the Flash content more usable and easy to send to others. As always, every part of the site will be printable.

+ careers +

Electronic Media Production Artist
We are looking for a detail-oriented production artist to create web pages, media for CD-ROM's and print-ready artwork. This unique opportunity allows you to work from home. Annual salary is approximately 35K, depending on experience.
Creative requirements include the ability work with designers to produce media content based on approved designs and project specifications. Some original design work may be necessary. Production requirements include significant experience with Dreamweaver (or other HTML-based production software), Flash, Photoshop, Image Ready, and Fireworks. Experience with Illustrator and InDesign are also desirable. Preferential consideration will be given to applicants with a home office.
In addition to a competitive salary, we offer an equipment stipend and full benefits.

###

Sales Representatives:
If you are a self-sufficient, successful sales person who can take

FIGURE 7-6

Careers page before redesign

Print Page

+ careers +

Electronic Media Production Artist
We are looking for a detail-oriented production artist to create web
pages, media for CD-ROM's and print-ready artwork. This unique
opportunity allows you to work from home. Annual salary is approximately 35K, depending on experience.
Creative requirements include the ability work with designers to
produce media content based on approved designs and project specifications. Some original design work may be necessary.
Production requirements include significant experience with Dreamweaver (or other HTML-based production software), Flash, Photoshop, Image Ready, and Fireworks. Experience with Illustrator and
InDesign are also desirable. Preferential consideration will be given
to applicants with a home office.
In addition to a competitive salary, we offer an equipment stipend and
full benefits.

Recommend To Friend   Apply For Job

###
Sales Representatives:
If you are a self-sufficient, successful sales person who can take

FIGURE 7-7

Careers page after redesign

Summary

We hope this example has illustrated the types of usability problems common
in Flash-based sites and the ways in which these problems can be overcome.
By providing real-world solutions that work from both the design and
usability perspectives, we hope to prove that form and function can coexist
in Flash development.

Flash developers should be keenly aware of usability and how it affects the content of a site. Flash interface design should always support and enhance the content, not detract from it. Flash offers developers much more control over layout and design than HTML. The greatest benefit Flash offers is the capability to produce interactive elements and animation without the problems associated with traditional HTML. Flash brings Iconideas.com to life in a way traditional HTML could never do. Clients demand more interesting content, but they shouldn't sacrifice good content for usability.

Usability testing is key
when developing human
interfaces, and a very
important element of
creating effective Flash
content.
–Kevin Lynch, Macromedia

chapter **8**

The Future of Flash

In Chapter 6, you learned how to test your Flash content for delivery. In this chapter, you learn how the delivery and execution of your content will change in the future. We discuss the future of Flash and how it will evolve with the Microsoft .Net strategy. We interview application services providers to discover how they're using Flash in their web application strategies. We explore how Flash is being used as an interface to sophisticated back-end database systems that supply large corporations with mission-critical data. Finally, we examine the concept of rethinking Flash not strictly as a web page–animation tool, but as a connective hub that behaves like a web browser and media, all at the same time.

Flash as Front End to Web Services

Flash has amazing potential as a full-blown development tool for creating applications online. To understand the future, you must review the past.

In the early 1980s, Video Works Interactive was used to create multimedia applications, business presentations, kiosks, and CD-ROMs. Video Works, later known as Director, became the standard development tool for creating a wide variety of applications used in different media. With the easy-to-use, but robust, Lingo scripting language, Director could be used to create applications that behaved more and more like programs written in C or C++. As the popularity of the Internet increased, Macromedia developed Shockwave content that could play within web pages. Although Shockwave content was highly compressed compared to its offline counterparts, it still contained large file sizes that were prohibitive to 14.4K and 56K modem users. Shockwave content enjoyed success, but it did not become the standard in web interactivity or animation.

In the mid 1990s, Macromedia purchased the company that created FutureSplash, and later renamed the product as Flash. Flash got a major boost when Microsoft used it to create interface and animation elements for the Microsoft site. Many developers saw Microsoft using this new animation tool and it was given creditability in the still-growing web development community.

Director evolved from a tool that primarily handled video and animation to a tool that could be used to display complex data, such as databases, and to serve chat rooms on the Internet. Flash is also following this same path. Flash started its life primarily as an animation tool, much like Director, but is now being used for much more. *Director* is the industry standard for creating interactive applications on DVD-ROM, CD-ROM, and kiosks. *Flash* is the industry standard for displaying interactive content online. As Director evolved, it was, in some ways, limited by the media on which it was delivered. Robust Director applications required considerable disk space. Often projectors and the associated DIR movie files would easily consume over 100 megabytes of space on a CD-ROM. Also, the physical limitations of delivering CD-ROMs required you to have a physical copy of the media to use the application. Unlike Director, Flash didn't suffer from these limitations as it developed. Flash started as a medium designed to be distributed over a network. This gave Flash the capability to reach more users faster, without the need for users to have physical media, such as a CD-ROM, to play it.

With the increase in the functionality of ActionScript and the creation of tools such as Macromedia Generator, Flash can now perform many complex actions, much as Director did years earlier. Flash can use server-side and client-side processing to delegate the processing of specific tasks. Flash can render interface elements in the browser window, while sending commands to have the server perform actions such as database queries or drawing complex weather maps using Generator. The future lies in Flash's capability to harness back-end processes and display them in graphically rich and interactive interfaces. Flash is the right media at the right time. As applications become more distributed, Flash is positioned to be the standard interface development tool for web applications.

Q & A   Interview with Rob Cleveland, Flash and ASP Developer

Rob, tell us a little about your experience and background as an ASP developer.

ICON has been developing web-based software and offering it to major corporate clients well before an acronym was assigned to the task. Essentially, the breakthrough in all web-based systems started with the first dbase connectivity. When we mastered this, more than five years ago, the entire picture changed. We knew at that point a major shift in how software would function had emerged.

How have you used Flash for intranet applications?

We have started exploring methods to use Flash that enables users to manipulate information in ways that simply are not possible with HTML. These applications still are limited, not by the technology, but by the acceptance of IT/IS departments who are wary of any major shift in web technologies.

What do you think is the biggest challenge for ASP developers regarding using Flash for the front end to their web services?

The corporate customer still has a certain "plug-in" phobia when it comes to real, enterprise-level application development. No matter how much data we bring to customers on Flash integration, they still are nervous about users having to manage their local clients. And then there's the cost. Right now, ASPs can develop applications using dynamic pages that really hit home when it comes to return on investment. When you start looking at Flash, it becomes a more complex, and costly, proposition.

How do you feel Flash has made interfaces more usable for web applications?

It is a completely different ballgame. With Flash, we can literally reinvent the operating environment. There are no constraints. We are totally free to apply information and functionality based on our vision. I think that inherently makes Flash interfaces more usable if we are thinking up front about the users and how they can effectively execute their required tasks.

When you present the idea of using Flash as a delivery format to a client, what approach do you use to help sell the benefits?

We try to help them understand the control they will have in creating the operating environment. It is a tough sell, though. Many customers still are ramping up web-based applications and simply aren't ready to take another major leap forward.

Does using Flash reduce or increase development time when building web applications? Why?

Initially, there is an increase in development time as programmers and designers reach a higher level of core competency. Ultimately, I think the cost will remain higher, not because it's harder, but because the possibilities are greater. Clients tend to gravitate toward those options that are most difficult to deliver.

Where do you see Flash evolving in the future?

It depends. Other solutions on the horizon like XML will offer greater flexibility in terms of information distribution and functionality over the Web. This format will certainly handle some of the usability issues that manifest with current HTML technology. But XML isn't much easier than Flash and it, too, has limitations. Unfortunately, Flash isn't an "open" resource or a standard that everyone can embrace. If Macromedia looks ahead and tries to establish Flash as a standard on par with XML, I believe it could be a universal toolset.

Do you think Flash will find a home in the Microsoft .Net strategy?

I doubt it. Microsoft has a colossal "not invented here" syndrome. To embrace a technology made popular by a major software competitor is almost taboo in Redmond. Unfortunately, Microsoft will probably create its own proprietary system to deliver web-based software functionality. And, if I had to bet a dollar, I would guess its system would be vector-based and have striking similarities to Flash.

Where Are Flash and Broadband Going?

Flash and broadband have a bright future together. Flash is evolving as broadband becomes more prevalent. As broadband becomes widespread, Internet media services will deliver richer media, and areas that will benefit from this fatter pipe will be entertainment sites. Imagine in the future that, instead of going to a store to rent a video, you will simply enter your credit card at a web site and begin to watch the movie of your choice on your "media appliance." Microsoft is already developing a media box that will enable users to watch movies, play games, and control household appliances from one unit. Flash will play a vital role in the delivery of broadband entertainment, news, and information. If Flash continues to develop on its current path, it will become the essential ingredient that helps the browser glue many different types of rich content together. Video, 3-D objects, and other types of media can be displayed using rich interfaces created in Flash.

Flash in broadband also has benefits for the advertising industry. Animated banner ads are becoming ineffective. Studies show users ignore them, and the click-through rate is sometimes so low companies can barely justify spending already tight advertising dollars on such things. Banner ads are simply too boring. Consumers expect exciting commercials with music and interesting effects. Because of the use of special effects and good sound production, television commercials can be minimovies, which are more effective at holding the consumer's attention. Using Flash and broadband, advertising agencies will again be able to start building minimovies that will engage users and won't be as boring or static as animated GIF banner ads.

Imagine an Internet where bandwidth is no longer an issue, and where the lines separating static web pages, television, and interactive applications blur. The idea of a page or a static piece of information has been totally changed because of Flash's layering capability. Content can now be displayed in pieces or mixed together to form new content by the end user. The booklike model of "turning" a page to read more information has been surpassed. Using Flash, developers can layer information and design in a way that wasn't possible with traditional HTML.

In the future, as bandwidth becomes less of an issue, we will see the Internet and television marry. The child of these two technologies will be a hyperactive, hyperreal feast for the senses. This is the inevitable course for two forms of media that need each other. Internet content, even with the current iteration of Flash, still lacks the rich media of television. And television, with all its rich visuals and sounds, is rather stupid compared to its smarter friend, the Internet. This new media type will be a sensory-

Q & A Interview with Steven Car, Art Director for Chevrolet.com

Steve, please give us some information on your background.

I'm a digital art supervisor for an ad agency and have been working in the digital field for approximately five years. Prior to this, my background includes 11 years of graphic design and computer support. I've developed many web sites that include the use of Flash technology from initial concept to final development. Some of these sites have won local advertising awards, for example for Chevrolet (2000 Monte Carlo prelaunch, 2000 Corvette, and 2000 Tahoe web sites).

What has Flash enabled you to do with Chevrolet.com that has enhanced the user experience?

For a company like Chevrolet, which has a diverse lineup of vehicles, they have to advertise to a variety of different markets and to a wide range of ages, from teenagers to senior citizens. Each vehicle has its own unique "branding" associated with it. By using Flash technology, I have the tool needed to make custom sites or modules that have a unique personality, relating to both their TV and print advertising.

Have you had experience with interactive Flash banner ads? How do you think Flash banners ads will evolve in the future?

Personally, I haven't created any Flash banners. But, I do think they are much more dynamic than the typical animated GIFs. I think an increase in the frequency of Flash banners is a good thing for the future. But, when you start seeing more of the ads that "float" over page content, that seems like it could annoy someone more than entertain them.

How do you think the advertising industry will use interactive media such as Flash in the future?

I see Flash modules used as demonstrations of various products as the best use for the advertising industry. Combine that with an integrated ad campaign that supports the demonstration (such as a print piece referring users to the web module) and this gives the consumer a more complete experience with the product. That, in turn, would give the client a greater chance for another sale.

If you had a wish list for features added to Flash for the future, what would they be?

I'd like to see some timing control, similar to Director's. I'd also like to see some instant animation features. I think they're adding something like that to the next version, though.

How do you plan to use Flash in future work you're doing for Chevrolet.com?

If a product has a cool, new feature the client wants to promote heavily within its site, we'll be doing more interactive modules, rich-media e-mail blasts, as well as future vehicle launches that would demand Flash-ier introductions.

Do you think Flash-driven web sites and traditional television programming are going to merge in the future? How will this change how the advertising industry does business?

I think this all depends on broadband expansion in the future. Once the majority of users have broadband, the industry can then look to the Web as an option for broadcast advertising.

What trends do you see the advertising industry following for the next few years regarding the use of Flash online?

I believe this depends on two things: (1) the product and (2) the target market. If you're shopping for a car, usually you want to get as much product information and as many facts as you can. Building a Flash site just for this reason might not be the best idea, especially if the majority of information is pulled from a central database. Perhaps using minimal Flash elements would be the answer here. Also, if the market you're trying to reach isn't interested in animation or sound, Flash might not be as important to use.

What are your thoughts on how Flash has affected web developers?

I believe Flash has given web developers an excellent tool to extend their creative freedom. Even though Flash seems to require some degree of programming knowledge, depending on how far you take it, the flexibility and wide acceptance of Flash on the Web makes it a must-have for serious web developers.

energizing environment. It could possibly be a virtual reality environment, much like sci-fi movies such as *Lawnmower Man* or the classic *Tron.* Regardless of what technology is used to display this new media, it will definitely combine the interactivity of Flash and the robust media of television. This is the logical evolution of the two forms of media.

Where Is Flash Usability Going?

As the complexity of interactive media grows, developers must be more familiar with how to create usable Flash sites. Web sites are quickly becoming an important extension of an organization's digital storefront. A variety of organizations—from Fortune 500 companies to international charities—are now using web sites to do business and relate to their clients. This digital storefront is often more than a secondary means to interface with a brick-and-mortar company; it can even be the only interface. Software companies, such as Macromedia, are now offering electronic purchase of their products. Consumers can now purchase copies of the software that don't include any physical shipment. This makes designing a highly usable interface even more important because clients are only interacting with the digital storefront. A poorly designed site can lead directly to lower sales. Flash is being used more and more as an interface for users to experience a product online. For example, users can rotate objects and zoom in on cloths to see the fabric texture. This heightened level of sensory experience with products enables e-tailers to showcase products that often didn't sell well online before.

How the public interacts with these Flash modules is critical to the success of the site. A hard-to-use interface could frustrate users, sending them away without making a purchase. Flash developers might be held accountable for the lack of usability of a Flash site. Any damages caused because of poor usability and reduced profits could cause legal problems for the Flash developer. When it comes to developing usable content for mission-critical applications, Flash developers would be wise to ensure usability is the number one focus of their efforts.

Flash Usability and the Multifaceted Team

In the past few years, Flash has grown from a tool primarily used by web designers to a tool used by a multifaceted team of individuals. Flash's robust animation capabilities have drawn users from the animation world, such as cartoonists and 3-D animators. Hard-core programmers have also adopted

Flash as an alternative to clunky Java applets that display weather and other data. University professors are using Flash as a cost-effective way to deliver teaching materials both over the Web and in a classroom presentation. Often on large projects, many different types of people are involved in the production of Flash content. With so many different skill sets involved, it becomes even more important to address usability.

As our online systems become more complex, it will be critical for companies to hire specialists who can coordinate how information is displayed and used. Many larger companies hire information architects and usability specialists, but smaller companies are still trying to "wing it" by having their graphic designer or project manager attempt to address usability issues in project planning and development. These types of sites are becoming easier and easier to spot when they're compared to sites that had the benefit of usability analysis and development. Many information architects are coming from the fields of library and information science, and the schools teaching these disciplines are slowly changing the curriculum to keep pace with the changing technology. As more classes of students graduate with this specialized knowledge, the Flash community will change because developers have more contact with usability and information design specialists.

Flash Is More Than Animation or a Page

Flash can no longer be defined as a tool for creating animation and interactivity because it no longer is a simple object that displays on a page. Flash has evolved through many creative uses into all these things at once. Flash can display linear and nonlinear objects in the same space. Because of Flash's unique capability to change form so quickly, many Flash developers have created usability problems due to their lack of experience with such media. Many developers come from a graphic design background, and others have roots in animation and video editing. Flash presents many challenges to usability that neither group has ever encountered. How do these developers deal with a media type that can easily morph from one state (a static page) to the other (animation)? As Flash becomes more widely used, developers from other fields will need to rely on the expertise of usability experts to help guide their projects.

Personal Viewpoint
How I Came to Care About Information Architecture

My first contact with an information architect wasn't exactly a good one. I was designing a web site for a local automotive supplier. I had been designing sites for several years and had a systematic approach to my method, which didn't include taking direction on how to lay out or even label my navigation toolbar by anyone except the client and sometimes a creative director.

As I began this project, I was told by the project manager that I needed to meet with the information architect assigned to the project. So, we met and she presented me with a site map outlining the content and its labels. At first, I thought this would be make my job easier. I would no longer have to think about what to name sections or how to organize the navigation bar. Later, I discovered how much I had to change my way of thinking to help build a usable web site.

As I developed the look and feel for the project, I decided I wanted a clean and minimal interface. The navigation toolbar text items were long. When I designed the toolbar with all the text items, it looked busy, distracting the user from the content. I decided to hide the navigation elements into a drop-down form.

I presented my design idea to the internal team and the information architect didn't like the hidden drop-down menu. The information architect told me the user group wouldn't be able to use the navigation as easily as it could if the menu items weren't hidden. I argued with the information architect that creating a traditional navigation bar would deviate from my design ideas. We reviewed the target audience and she explained the target audience was a less-technically savvy computer crowd. Hiding the navigation would only increase the chances the users might miss the navigation (the most important part of the site). I agreed to change my design.

Designing a clean-looking interface with such long names for each section was a challenge, but I accomplished my goal. I was frustrated about being told to change my design. I thought the drop-down menu was easy to use. My attitude was this: if the users didn't know how to use the drop-down menu, then they shouldn't have a computer. I think this type of attitude is also prevalent among other designers. We often get caught up in our world of design as "king" and put on blinders for more important global issues. What good was my amazing design if the users couldn't use the site? Obviously, I wasn't thinking of my target audience. I was so caught up in creating good design, I lost sight of the original goal: creating an easy-to-use and well-designed site.

As designers working for corporations, we try to drill as much creative energy into the blue borders of our corporate design as possible, and I believe designers need to readdress this attitude. I think we need to draw a line in our minds between our agenda and the needs of the site and the client. We need to refocus our energies on to how to design more usable interfaces—especially in Flash—yet maintain a high level of creativity at the same time. Often, these are the challenges that produce better design in the end. For me, it's a creative challenge to make a Flash site highly usable, yet highly creative at the same time. The balance between form and function is always precarious.

–Kevin Airgid

Q & A Interview with Sebastien Chevrel from Second Story

Please give us some information on your background and experience using Flash.

I've been involved in graphics and multimedia programming for over ten years and have focused on web technologies for the last six years. I started experimenting with Flash on my personal web site (http://www.seb.cc) a couple of years ago and got heavily involved with it when I joined Second Story (http://www.secondstory.com) in October 2000.

In all the projects you've worked on, which stick out in your mind as examples of highly usable Flash interfaces?

Although considerable controversy surrounds Flash and usability or, more precisely, accessibility, I think Flash enables us to enhance the user's experience by challenging the traditional way a user interacts and by custom-tailoring an interface to respond to a particular problem or set of data. This is a double-edged sword because nontraditional interfaces and modes of interaction might be harder to use at first, but once a user has figured them out, I believe they greatly enhance the experience.

Here are two examples:

The Museum of Modern Art, "Artists of Brücke: Themes in German Expressionist Prints" http://www.moma.org/brucke (specifically, the Prints section)

The Prints section enables you to view a thumbnail gallery of the entire collection of 100+ prints and filter the collection by Artist, Themes, and Mediums. Flash enabled us to darken prints that didn't match the query and highlight the ones that did, thus providing a strong visual feedback of the context of a particular query in relation to the whole collection. Although the interaction mode is fairly standard in this example (check boxes), the visual feedback is superior to what a traditional search/filter engine provides.

National Geographic Online, "Remembering Pearl Harbor" http://www.nationalgeographic.com/pearlharbor/ (specifically, the interactive attack map)

I want to highlight two elements of this project interface:

Reactive timeline   We needed to present a minute-by-minute sequence of the events. The challenge was the high density of events surrounding 7:55 A.M. (the time when the actual attack occurred), while presenting enough contextual information (from 3:42 A.M. to 1 P.M.) on that day. Our solution involved a reactive timeline that stretches and zooms in as your mouse gets closer to the center, where the events are dense, and zooms back out when you mouse over the edges.

Animated map In conjunction with the timeline, the information is contextualized geographically by plotting events on a map that animates (pans and zooms) as you move from one time marker to the next in the timeline.

Although this interface might seem a little intimidating at first, I think, ultimately, it provides the user with a lot of contextual information about the attack that would have been impossible to convey on the Web without Flash. The immediate feedback that such an interface provides is superior to the kind of interaction you might have with a normal HTML page and capitalizes on the way our brain interprets motion and visual information.

When you develop Flash interfaces, how do you ensure they're easy to use? How do you test the interfaces?

We usually work on what we call an "experience map" before beginning any visual design. The goal is to nail down the functionality of the application and how the user will navigate and experience the content. Once this is completed and approved by clients, we start to work on visual and interface design. I think this is a powerful way to approach a problem. Too often, visual design is developed simultaneously to the experience design, which leads to poorer usability because of conflicting goals.

We also always keep in mind interface design and usability best practices, and try to get as many people as possible to test our work and give us feedback. The interdisciplinary nature of our team helps, and client and end user feedback is key. We learn from every project and keep getting better at it.

What trends do you see for Flash design for the future? How will these trends affect usability?

I think that Flash will become more and more transparent, and less and less flashy. Flash is a powerful tool that enables you to create complex applications fairly easily, compared to traditional application programming.

The trend I'm most excited about is the idea of invisible interface or datacentric interfaces. This sort of work has been pioneered by user interface research labs, such as the Xerox Parc, the MIT Media Lab, and the University of Maryland, and is now making its way into the mainstream interface design via Flash. This is still somewhat at the experimentation level, but I think we'll see more and more of that in production web sites soon.

These sort of advances will require users to relearn how to do certain things when interacting with a web site but, in the end, the usability will be increased tremendously.

What usability issues would you like to see addressed in future versions of Flash?

I think usability is in the hands of the designers and programmers. There's little Flash can't do in this domain. Better rendering performance (especially on the Macintosh) can help because high-feedback latency decreases usability, but this is mostly a design issue.

On the topic of accessibility, which is related to usability, Flash has room to improve when it comes to printing and allowing publishers to export stripped-down versions of their work without double-building. I think Macromedia is working hard on this and we should see an improvement in the future.

As broadband becomes more widely used, how do you see media, such as television and the Internet, merging together? Where do you think Flash will fit into this picture?

We need to do better than merge television and the Internet. I think the passive experience of watching television will always have a place in our lives, while broadband will continue to enhance a more interactive approach.

Although bringing television-type content to the Web is a natural impulse (the first television shows were also inspired from the radio medium), we need to think outside the box and create something new. Flash is one tool, among others, to get the job done.

Second Story has worked on projects like Janet Jackson's web site in the past. How do you think entertainers and record labels will use Flash in the future?

Flash takes interaction and entertainment to a new level. In Janet Jackson's site, for example, we created a Soundboard Remixer that enables you to create your own remix of a song by moving sliders and knobs on a mixing table. We've had extremely positive feedback about it and this is exactly the sort of thing the Web and Flash can do: put the users in charge of making their own content and experience. The idea is to provide the tools, rather than the finished product. I see entertainment as being the first sector to widely adopt this sort of approach, but others will follow.

As you proceed to build new projects in the future, what things will you change about how you build Flash sites to make them more usable?

We always try to learn from our mistakes and from the feedback we get. But, I don't anticipate any major change in the way we approach usability. I think as this new breed of interfaces I mentioned earlier makes its way into the mainstream, users will start to get used to the approach and we'll be able to be more daring in pushing the envelope without scaring people off. It's always a fine line to navigate, but I think it will get easier to sell nonconventional approaches to clients in the future.

What advice would you give to Flash developers to help them build more usable sites?

The most important thing is not to fall into the trap of technology. Flash is only a tool, and good design, architecture, and thinking are paramount. Stay away from the eye candy and concentrate on what adds value to the user's experience. Challenge your preconceptions about usability and how a web site should work and what it should look like.

Flash a 100 Years from Now?

Imagine what the Internet will evolve into 100 years in the future. Imagine a world where nanotechnology has changed everything about our lives. We use nanotechnology as an example, but it could be some other type of technology that will change how the Internet evolves. For this discussion, it doesn't matter what technology becomes more widely used—we know for certain things will change, yet the goals of usability will remain the same. Imagine nanotechnology has progressed to a point where certain materials can be reshaped into new objects with the right instruction set. If you need a new watch, nanorobots can reshape the elements already available in your home into a new designer watch. To purchase this watch, you log into the global network. You might navigate this network through a three-dimensional holographic display or some type of neural connection that simulates reality in your brain (can you say *The Matrix*?). Regardless of the method you use, your goal is to obtain your new watch. Physical shipment isn't important anymore. The important and valuable commodity you desire is the information or instructions on how your nanobots can build your watch for you. Today, information is valuable, but in the future it will be the *only* commodity you purchase. You won't pay for the shipping and production of your watch, but you will pay for the engineering, style, and design.

Where does Flash fit into this picture? Flash has evolved into a highly advanced interface design tool that enables users to build this virtual storefront. Currently, interior designers, store display specialists, graphic designers, and many others are involved in creating the experience of shopping online. The main thread that ties these disciplines together is usability. Without an experience that has been tested and is easy to use, the work of all our talented specialists is for nothing. We use this science fiction example of the future to illustrate how usability is important. All the technology in the world won't solve usability problems. This takes common sense and the experience to understand how to build sites that are truly easy to use.

Usability Resources Online

The following resources represent excellent places to start when looking for additional information on Flash usablity. Most of these resources are updated regularly, with new techniques and source files to help make your Flash content more usable.

Flash 99% Good

http://www.flash99good.com/

This is the companion site to this book. Here, we feature updated links and tips and video tutorials on how to make Flash content more usable with real-world solutions. This site also features a gallery to give you ideas on how to merge good design and usability into a successful Flash project.

Macromedia Flash Usability

**http://www.macromedia.com/software/flash/
productinfo/usability/**

This site features many excellent links, white papers, and related articles on Flash usability. Macromedia also features a contest that provides real-world examples on how to improve usability in Flash.

Evolt.org

http://www.evolt.org/flash/

Evolt.org is a world community for web developers, promoting the mutual free exchange of ideas, skills, and experiences. This site features excellent articles on Flash usability.

Robert Penner

http://www.robertpenner.com

Robert Penner is a Canadian Flash developer who provides many excellent examples of advanced ActionScript source code. In particular, Robert provides an excellent script to enable Flash to use the browser's Back and Forward buttons.

Flash Kit

http://www.flashkit.com/

This site features open source Flash movies and tutorials on how to build better Flash content.

ActionScripts.org

http://www.actionscripts.org/

This site offers well-designed and easy-to-follow tutorials on how to eliminate many of the common Flash usability problems using simple ActionScripts.

Flash Magazine

http://www.flashmagazine.com/

This site is designed completely in Flash and is easy to use. It is not only a good example of a well-designed Flash site, it also offers good articles on Flash usability.

UltraShock

http://www.ultrashock.com

Another open source site that features high-quality Flash movies, tutorials, and news.

Shockfusion

http://www.shockfusion.com/

One of the first Flash-only message boards on the scene. The version 2.0 features many updated features and excellent areas to ask questions and post new sites for peer review.

uidesign.net

http://www.uidesign.net/

This site features excellent white papers on interface design and usability.

Flazoom

http://www.flazoom.com/usability/

An excellent article that describes Flash as a journey. Some great real-world examples are used in this article.

Flash Unusable Gallery

In the following section, we present a series of common Flash interfaces. This gallery represents styles of navigation that aren't easy to use. In each instance, we point out the problems with the navigation style and suggest ways to improve it, while maintaining the original design style.

Problem 1: Hidden Navigation

In this example (see Figure 8-1) we have the classic hidden navigation Flash menu. Many Flash designers use this type of design because it leaves the page clean looking and uncluttered. Unfortunately, it makes the site hard to use because users are forced to move their cursors over objects to understand what they link to. In this case, the buttons are small gray circles. This makes the problem even worse because the gray circles don't appear to look like buttons. Understanding that many users need things to be simple and easy to use is important. Common sense should play a role in the way you develop usable content. Try to make buttons look clickable. The second issue with this site is that all browser navigation has been removed. The Back button is the most frequently used part of the browser. Pop-up window Flash sites should be avoided.

Solution

The designer could make this navigation easier to use by labeling the buttons and applying some type of graphic treatment so they look more like buttons. This doesn't mean you need to add drop shadows and bevels. Find a way to make it obvious that an area is clickable, by color or by other graphic means. To keep this site clean, the designer might think about having the text labels slightly wrap around the circle buttons if the text labels are short. Or, maybe spread the buttons out further to create more white space.

Problem 2: Animating Buttons

Just because you can, doesn't mean you should. This applies to animating buttons in Flash. Creating complex animations when you roll over a button is not only annoying, it's old school. Animation should be used to enhance the message to your target audience. More often than not, mouse rollovers

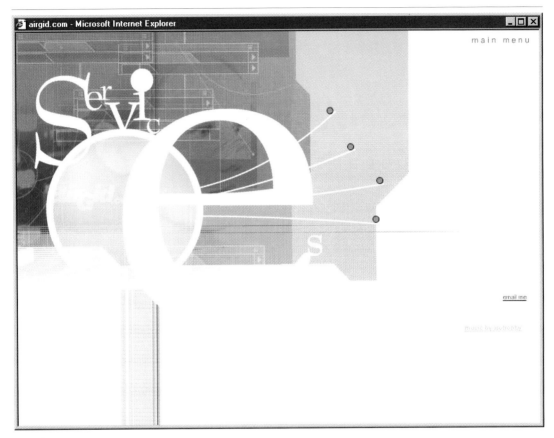

FIGURE 8-1

Classic hidden navigation

don't serve any purpose other than to annoy users. Try using a site like the example shown in Figure 8-2 for more than a minute. The animation of each button growing larger makes users feel they're running through quicksand to accomplish their goals. Sites like this often feature forced animation sequences that build the interface from one screen to the other. Once again, look at your target audience. Does the animation add value to your message or is it just something you want to do? Learn to distinguish your agenda from the goals of the target audience and the site.

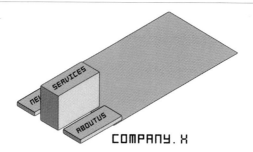

FIGURE 8-2

Out-of-control rollover buttons

Solution

Remove the growing 3-D bar and replace it with a color change or something less obtrusive. Less is more. Navigation design doesn't always have to be big and bad. The lack of images and negative space can also make a bold statement. Making things simple can often make the design and usability better.

Problem 3: The Splash Page

Splash pages are not recommended for most sites. Users don't benefit from having to skip over a splash page to get at the content. Anything that slows a user's access to content and their target is not a good idea. A splash page, however, can benefit a site in some instances; for example, multilanguage Flash sites can enable users to pick a language before they enter.

　　Too often, developers use the splash page as a means for users to download the Flash plug-in, as shown in Figure 8-3. These splash pages are busy and it's difficult for the user to know where to click, even to enter the site.

Solution

Don't use a splash page at all. If you need to include a splash page for your Flash site, make it simple and easy to understand. Clearly label the Enter button and make it the most prominent feature of the page. Make the hit zone bigger than anything else on the page. Don't rely on the fact that you warned users on the home page they need the latest version of the Flash plug-in. Use ActionScript to detect if the user has the correct version of Flash.

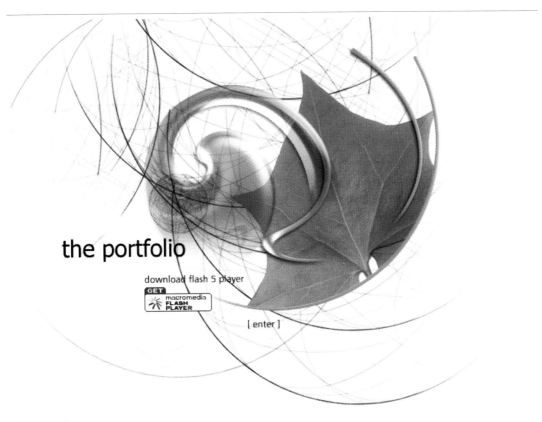

FIGURE 8-3

The busy splash page

Problem 4: Navigation Elements that Move and Are Hard to Read

Imagine you walked into an elevator, started to push the button for the floor you wanted, and the button moved away from your finger. This is the same frustration users feel when they come to sites that have navigation that moves by itself. Navigation elements should *never* move. And navigation systems should always use a clear font. Try to avoid script-type fonts for navigation, such as the one shown in Figure 8-4.

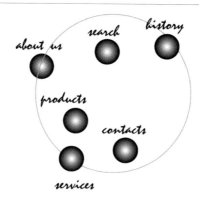

FIGURE 8-4

Moving navigation, with a hard-to-read font

Solution

Have the navigation items in a fixed location. Does it add value to your project to have navigation items float? The answer to this question 99 percent of the time is No. Try to use fonts with simple and easy characters for navigation labels. Do a little research. Ask people who wear glasses to review the navigation labels to ensure they're easy to read.

Problem 5: Small Hit Zones and Uniform Style

Many sites are now copying the style shown in Figure 8-5—the detail-oriented, highly complex interface, with small buttons whose small hit zones make finding content a nightmare. That this style has been copied over and over again should be reason enough not to use it. The second problem with this type of interface is that everything looks so similar. The buttons, the content, and the edges of the boxes all blend into one array of design, and it's difficult for the eye to follow where navigation ends and content begins, which makes using this site a chore. Another large usability issue with this type of site is the use of pixel fonts. Pixel fonts in themselves aren't bad, but setting text to 6 points and making it blend into the background makes type almost unreadable, even for people with good eyesight.

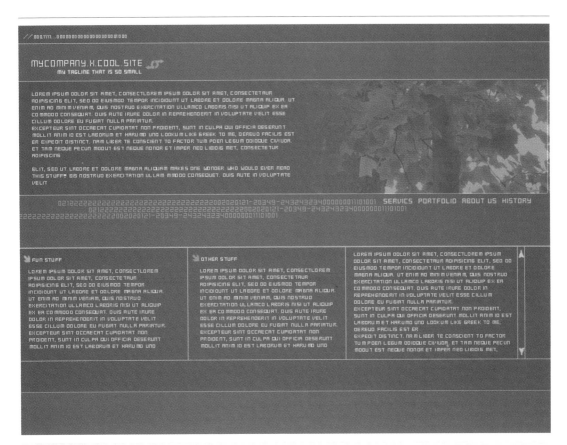

FIGURE 8-5

Everything looks the same in this interface

Solution

Try to make navigation easy to use and clearly labeled. This might sound like common sense, but make buttons look like buttons. Users shouldn't have to guess about navigation. Avoid using small fonts with little contrast. If you want your users to read something, make it clear and concise.

Q & A Interview with Kevin Lynch, Chief Software Architect of Macromedia

Please give us some information on your background and experience.

I've been designing and developing software for more than 20 years, and am currently chief software architect at Macromedia. In that role, I'm responsible for Macromedia's family of software, including Macromedia Flash, Dreamweaver, and ColdFusion, and for guiding our overall product strategy.

I was fortunate enough to have participated in the emergence of the personal computer from the late '70s through the graphical user interfaces of the '80s to the profoundly networked systems of today.

My work highlights include Macromedia Dreamweaver, Adobe FrameMaker, human interface design at General Magic for handheld personal communicators, the design of early Macintosh desktop publishing tools, the first Macintosh 3-D modeling application, and a graphical adventure game released in 1984. I studied interactive computer graphics at the University of Illinois, working with artists and engineers in the Electronic Visualization Laboratory. I believe the designs I work on are distinctive in their simplicity and depth, the basis for software that is practical, powerful, and enjoyable.

What is Macromedia's reply to comments such as "Flash is not usable"?

A tremendous amount of user-interface design innovation is happening in the Flash community and this results in a full range of work from world-class usability to designs that can be totally perplexing. This innovation and experimentation is the core of what moves the Internet forward and I believe will result in a far better experience for all of us longer term.

To make Flash content and the Internet in general more usable, we are working in partnership with the Macromedia user community to develop the techniques for designing great experiences and supporting these in our software to empower the whole community to leverage this experience.

We believe that content designed in Macromedia Flash can be the most usable on the Internet, and we are beginning to see this emerge already as more and more examples of good user experiences created with Flash appear every day from engaging information to powerful and efficient applications.

What do you think are the biggest strides Macromedia has made in terms of usability for the release of Flash MX?

We've focused on three areas for creating usable content in Macromedia Flash MX: the authoring experience, the player, and instructional material.

In the Flash MX authoring tool, we built in specific features to make the more usable choice the first choice. The best way to encourage usable content design is to make it easiest to author—for example, many Flash applications make use of a scroll bar in their design and, up to now, everyone had to build their own, which resulted in hundreds of different scroll bars that all behaved somewhat badly. In Flash MX, there is a scroll bar component that can be quickly dragged-and-dropped into a Flash design, which works great and will make it far easier to develop and customize the appearance without building from scratch. We've also created an open framework for the Macromedia community to build and exchange components with each other, which allows them to leverage their work and share the most usable design elements.

The Macromedia Flash Player has always been transparently integrated with web browsers, and being this invisible has been a usable approach for hundreds of millions of consumers. In the Flash Player, we furthered this transparent integration by enabling the standard bookmarks and Back button in the browser to control the Flash content. This will enable an even more usable experience for consumers using the user interface controls that are already familiar. We also made the Flash Player accessible through integration with screen readers and enabling accessible content to be easily created in the authoring environment.

Last, Macromedia has continually focused on providing resources to educate our designers about creating usable Macromedia Flash content. Flash MX builds on a lot of those resources, and contains specific features to try and make the usable choice the first choice. For example, components make usable content easier to reuse, as well as simplify the connection between Flash and web applications. Features in Flash MX also address accessibility, which seems to force people to think about usability in the process.

What usability issues is Macromedia going to challenge in future versions of Flash?

We will continue to add functionality to Flash that supports the best usability in the world, learning from the great experimentation being done by the Macromedia user community. We will also continue to communicate and increase awareness of the importance of usability, accessibility, and great experiences across devices and platforms.

How do you judge if a Flash site is successful from a usability standpoint?

Usability testing is key when developing human interfaces and an important element of creating effective Flash content. You have to try it on humans to see what works and what doesn't, and the best way is to see what your users are able and unable to do with your content. From this, you can typically determine if users are both happy with and successful on your site. You can do usability testing without a big investment and many resources are available online to help you do this.

As bandwidth becomes less of an issue, where do you feel Flash will be in five years?

We have always aimed to make it possible to deliver an experience that feels like high bandwidth over low-bandwidth connections using Flash. Those of us who have high-bandwidth connections at home or work are living in the future—it will still be a long time before the majority of people have high-bandwidth connections, and even with high bandwidth, efficient content delivery will be an issue.

Flash MX provides new features such as video support, as well as streaming audio and real-time conferencing that will definitely benefit from high bandwidth and provide some exciting new opportunities for everyone. The important thing for Flash development, as more and more people get faster connections, is for all of us to learn how to author scalable content that provides a great experience for low-bandwidth users and an even more engaging one for high-bandwidth users, without troubling the user with lots of decisions about which experience they want.

Of course, in five years, Macromedia Flash will have some even more exciting capabilities that I'm sure will benefit from high-bandwidth connections!

How do you think television and the Internet will merge into a new medium? Where does Flash fit into this scenario?

A tug of war is going on between companies that want the television to merge with the computer, as well as other companies that are trying to bring the computer into television sets. This is a philosophical war that hasn't been resolved yet. The good news is both sides are using Macromedia Flash as an important way to bridge these worlds, so, either way, Flash developers will have some great new opportunities. Flash is unparalleled in terms of expressiveness and consistency of experience, which is why Flash user interfaces are being used in set-top box platforms from Microsoft WebTV to Moxi and Liberate. Having Flash support in set-top boxes also empowers Flash designers to create new, as well as repurpose old, content to take advantage of these new markets.

What role, if any, will Flash have in the Microsoft .Net strategy?

Macromedia Flash Player is the only third-party player that ships with Microsoft Windows XP and it will work well with Microsoft .Net. Flash is complementary to .Net and will provide a great way to design user experiences that connect into the .Net world, leveraging XML Web Services and other Microsoft application technologies.

How does Macromedia plan to integrate Flash with more of its other products?

This is something we've been doing continually. Flash 5 objects could be created natively within Dreamweaver 4, and even further Flash integration will occur with future versions of Dreamweaver and ColdFusion. Flash will also be used for user interface elements within our upcoming tools and Flash panels will be used to extend the user interface of some of our future products.

If you could give advice to Flash developers regarding usability for future sites, what would it be?

Think about your design and how it relates to the end user. Test your design with live users. Reuse components whenever possible. Learn from experimentation and other effective Flash content. Stay on top of the application development space, as more sites evolve from browsing to doing. And, most important, keep enhancing the content to continually address these needs. Here are ten tips to developing great usable Flash content:

Tip 1: Remember User Goals   Users typically come to a site with a goal in mind. Each link and click should meet their expectations and lead them toward their goal. When streaming your site, have key navigation links appear first, in case the user wants to get to another area in the site. Emulating common GUI elements will increase usability.

Tip 2: Remember Site Goals   Site design should reflect business or client needs, effectively communicating the main message and promoting the brand. Yet, site goals are best achieved by respecting the user experience, so site structure should reflect user needs, quickly leading the user to their goal and avoiding company or regional jargon.

Tip 3: Avoid Unnecessary Intros   Although intro animations are exciting, they often delay the user's access to the information they seek. Always offer users either a Skip Intro command or alternative access to your home page. On their second visit to your home page, skip the intro animation altogether (use a client-side JavaScript cookie to accomplish this), and then on the destination page, give the option of returning to the animation.

Tip 4: Provide Logical Navigation and Interactivity   Keep the user oriented: Display the previous location and guide users to their next one. Remind users where they've been by programming links to change color after they're visited.

Give users an easy exit from each major section of the site and an easy return to their starting point.

Clearly indicate each link's destination. Keep navigation structures and nomenclature visible, rather than hiding them until the user has triggered an event (such as a mouseover).

Make sure your buttons have well-defined hit areas.

Display primary site navigational elements first by using the streaming capabilities of Macromedia Flash.

Support Back button navigation. To do this using built-in browser forward and back navigation, separate Flash movies into logical chunks, and then place them on individual HTML pages. Or, set up the movie to include a Flash-based Back button the user can use to return to a frame or scene that represents a logical previous page.

Tip 5: Design for Consistency   Consistency in user interface is the best way to improve your site's performance. Reusing architecture elements, design elements, and naming conventions frees the user's attention for your message as they navigate to their goal and it also aids site maintenance. You can use Smart Clips to reuse interactive elements throughout the site, and have words and images from initial navigation links reappear on destination pages.

Tip 6: Don't Overuse Animation   Avoid unnecessary animations. The best animations reinforce the site's goals, tell a story, or aid in navigation. Repeated animations on text-heavy pages distract the eye from the message of the page.

Tip 7: Use Sound Sparingly   Sound should enhance your site, but not be indispensable. For example, use sound to indicate the user has just triggered an event. Always provide on, off, and volume control onscreen, and remember, sound significantly increases file size. When you do use sound, Macromedia Flash will compress music into small MP3 files and even stream it.

Tip 8: Target Low-Bandwidth Users   The smaller the download, the better. The initial screen download should be no more than 40K, including all Macromedia Flash files, HTML, and images. To reduce download time, use smaller vector-based images (unless the image is a complex bitmap, in which case it's better left as a bitmap file), and use the Load Movie action only when the user specifically requests a file. If a wait is unavoidable, provide a load time sequence with a progress indicator and have navigation load in the first five seconds whenever possible.

Tip 9: Design for Accessibility   Make your content available to all users, including those with disabilities. Highly descriptive Alternate tags allow your content to be interpreted by assistive technology. The magnifying Smart Clip for zoom is another easy-to-use Macromedia Flash feature that allows more users to see your content. For an in-depth discussion about making Macromedia Flash content accessible, see the Macromedia Flash Accessibility site at http://www.macromedia.com/software/flash/productinfo/usability/.

Tip 10: Test for Usability   Have someone with fresh eyes test-drive your site to make sure it accomplishes both user and site goals. Even compact Macromedia Flash animations can delay users from reaching their goal, so use Macromedia Flash's built-in Bandwidth Profiler (located in the View menu in Test Movie mode) to analyze how well your site will perform over various bandwidths. Retest the site each time you make even small changes. Make sure your site testers match the demographic of your site's anticipated audience—especially if the anticipated audience includes users at various levels of comfort with site navigation.

Index

INTERNATIONAL CONTACT INFORMATION

AUSTRALIA
McGraw-Hill Book Company Australia Pty. Ltd.
TEL +61-2-9417-9899
FAX +61-2-9417-5687
http://www.mcgraw-hill.com.au
books-it_sydney@mcgraw-hill.com

CANADA
McGraw-Hill Ryerson Ltd.
TEL +905-430-5000
FAX +905-430-5020
http://www.mcgrawhill.ca

GREECE, MIDDLE EAST,
NORTHERN AFRICA
McGraw-Hill Hellas
TEL +30-1-656-0990-3-4
FAX +30-1-654-5525

MEXICO (Also serving Latin America)
McGraw-Hill Interamericana Editores S.A. de C.V.
TEL +525-117-1583
FAX +525-117-1589
http://www.mcgraw-hill.com.mx
fernando_castellanos@mcgraw-hill.com

SINGAPORE (Serving Asia)
McGraw-Hill Book Company
TEL +65-863-1580
FAX +65-862-3354
http://www.mcgraw-hill.com.sg
mghasia@mcgraw-hill.com

SOUTH AFRICA
McGraw-Hill South Africa
TEL +27-11-622-7512
FAX +27-11-622-9045
robyn_swanepoel@mcgraw-hill.com

UNITED KINGDOM & EUROPE
(Excluding Southern Europe)
McGraw-Hill Education Europe
TEL +44-1-628-502500
FAX +44-1-628-770224
http://www.mcgraw-hill.co.uk
computing_neurope@mcgraw-hill.com

ALL OTHER INQUIRIES Contact:
Osborne/McGraw-Hill
TEL +1-510-549-6600
FAX +1-510-883-7600
http://www.osborne.com
omg_international@mcgraw-hill.com